BEFORE AIDS

POLITICS AND CULTURE IN MODERN AMERICA

Series Editors:
Margot Canaday, Glenda Gilmore, Michael Kazin,
Stephen Pitti, Thomas J. Sugrue

Volumes in the series narrate and analyze political and social change
in the broadest dimensions from 1865 to the present, including ideas
about the ways people have sought and wielded power in the public
sphere and the language and institutions of politics at all levels—local,
national, and transnational. The series is motivated by a desire to reverse
the fragmentation of modern U.S. history and to encourage synthetic
perspectives on social movements and the state, on gender, race, and labor,
and on intellectual history and popular culture.

BEFORE AIDS

Gay Health Politics in the 1970s

Katie Batza

PENN

UNIVERSITY OF PENNSYLVANIA PRESS

PHILADELPHIA

Published by
University of Pennsylvania Press
Philadelphia, Pennsylvania 19104-4112
www.upenn.edu/pennpress

Printed in the United States of America on acid-free paper

10 9 8 7 6 5 4 3 2 1

Library of Congress Cataloging-in-Publication Data

Names: Batza, Katie, author.
Title: Before AIDS: gay health politics in the 1970s / Katie Batza.
Other titles: Politics and culture in modern America.
Description: 1st edition. | Philadelphia: University of Pennsylvania Press,
    [2018] | Series: Politics and culture in modern America | Includes
    bibliographical references and index.
Identifiers: LCCN 2017036427 | ISBN 9780812250138 (hardcover: alk. paper)
Subjects: LCSH: Gays—Medical care—United States—History—20th century. |
    Sexual minorities—Medical care—United States—History—20th century. |
    Gay liberation movement—United States—History—20th century.
Classification: LCC RA564.9.H65 B38 2018 | DDC 362.1086/64—dc23
LC record available at https://lccn.loc.gov/2017036427

To Kellie and Elliot,
life's best dance partners

CONTENTS

ABBREVIATIONS

GCSCP Gay Community Services Center Papers,
   ONE Archive, Los Angeles

GH Gerber/Hart Library and Archives, Chicago

HPA History Project Archives, Boston

MA Mazer Archives, Los Angeles

MKP Morris Kight Papers, 1975–1993, Department of Special
   Collections, Young Research Library, University of California,
   Los Angeles

OA ONE Archive, Los Angeles

SL Schlesinger Library, Radcliffe Institute, Harvard University,
   Boston

WLPC Walter Lear Personal Collection, Philadelphia

The Holiday Club's large sign, which encased the top quarter of the building and consisted of colorful, shimmering dish-sized sequins, made the architecture of the Howard Brown Health Center, which sat across the street at the corner of Irving Park and North Sheridan, especially unremarkable. The center first came to my attention as a building (not even an organization) in 2002 with the onset of my first Chicago winter, when I realized its gray concrete and muted tile façade provided a shield from the winter wind off Lake Michigan as I walked to and from the "El" stop closest to my apartment. Having grown up in Atlanta, I had never experienced an upper midwestern winter but quickly learned that wind defense during a six-block walk warranted switching to the other side of the street. Thus I abandoned the colorful Holiday Club for the more protected, if drab, Howard Brown building. As I became better acquainted with my new city, I learned that the Howard Brown Health Center served the LGBTQ community specifically, and the building I had come to think of fondly as my personal windshield was just one of the organization's many outposts. Curiosity piqued, I began to spend my long and solitary commutes imagining the organization's origins and how it fit into to my growing understanding of Chicago's LGBTQ geography and history. In this way, the breathtakingly cold and beautiful winters of Chicago combined with the sturdy impermeability of a serendipitously located health clinic to inspire what eventually became this book.

Before conducting any research, I imagined that Howard Brown originated in the Chicago gay community's response to the AIDS crisis. I assumed the same to be true of other well-known clinics serving the LGBTQ community around the country, including Whitman-Walker in Washington, D.C., New York's Callen-Lorde, and Boston's Fenway. My daydreamed history charted the birth and growth of gay medical clinics and research institutions amid bleak national fiscal and political realities, a gay sexual culture that equated sexual health with sexual oppression, and one of the deadliest epidemics in history. The plot unfolded in my mind like a bizarre historian's telenovela with conjectured tragedy and fantasized heroism, not to mention political drama and a fantastic soundtrack. It transformed my commute from an hour-long battle against motion sickness and claustrophobia into something far more interesting.

After many weeks of crafting this surmised history during bumpy and noisy train rides without even so much as a Google search worth of research, I decided that my fascination warranted a study of how gay community health clinics factored into the early response to AIDS. In the initial stages of research, I found that many gay community clinics actually originated in the 1970s, most of them in the last few years of the decade, but some dating back as early as 1971—a full decade before the first identified AIDS case. This realization left me wondering how these clinics came to be and just what gay clinics did before AIDS. That was the moment that my daydreamed commuter entertainment transformed into a real research project, the moment of conception for *Before AIDS*.

FIGHTING EPIDEMICS AND IGNORANCE

On a cold Chicago day in the mid-1970s, an employee of Man's Country, the largest bathhouse in the Midwest, lay in a hospital bed recuperating from a bad bout of hepatitis B. Though doctors and scientists hadn't yet discovered that hepatitis B could be transmitted sexually, the disease plagued the gay community. Gay men avoided interactions with doctors, however, because such visits often led to misdiagnosis, judgment, ostracism, and treatment for their sexuality rather than their medical ailments. In addition, medical care was often expensive and held the possibility of extortion, since gay men typically paid for their health care out of pocket and avoided using insurance for fear that employers would learn of their sexuality and then harass or fire them. Thus this particular patient was hardly the first gay man to appear at Chicago's Rush Presbyterian Hospital with the flu-like symptoms and slight yellowing of the skin that signified untreated hepatitis B. In fact, on this day, he even shared a room with a friend, another gay man suffering from the same illness. Like many others before and after them, both men worried how their sexuality might influence the medical staff or their treatment and felt their vulnerability amplified by their dependence on these potentially threatening care providers. They were sick and required treatment but had a healthy and well-founded apprehension about those designated to care for them.

But on this day, a nurse of a different sort, a representative of a growing gay health network in the city, lifted their spirits and allayed their fears. Drag performer Stephen Jones from Man's Country, dressed as stage persona Nurse Wanda Lust, made a special visit to the patients, one of whom remembered in an interview later, "All of a sudden, I was laying in my room, and there was

Nurse Lust walking through the halls of Rush Presbyterian Hospital [*laughs*], you know, ten feet tall, and just made no bones about being who he was."[1] Donning a short and tight-fitting nurse's uniform, a large oversized clock necklace, fake glasses, a bright red wig, high heels, and a nurse's hat and hairnet, Nurse Lust arrived to deliver flowers, check blood pressure, and visit with friends. As Nurse Lust walked the halls the patients could hear the hospital nurses giggle as she teased them playfully. The act of visiting in drag proved a potent tool that put the patients at ease but also signified to the hospital staff that gay patients had a community looking out for them. Nurse Wanda Lust acted as an advocate, an ambassador, and a friend in the exact spaces where gay men felt most vulnerable and threatened, and in doing so, she played an important role in changing the relationship gay men had to health care and to sexual health in the 1970s. Remembering Lust's visit, one person reflected, "He was freedom, in my head. Outrageous could work if you made people laugh and have fun with them. . . . Wanda was one of those people that helped make me feel good about my life."[2] Though Nurse Lust did not visit every gay patient every day, the fact that she visited at all marked a significant shift in attitudes about medical authority, gay health, and the right to quality health care that demonstrates the true importance of the gay health activism of the 1970s.

Like many other minority communities in the 1970s, gay men faced public health challenges that resulted as much from their political marginalization and social stigmatization as from any virus or disease. The incidence of venereal disease (VD) among the adult population of the United States grew to epidemic proportions in the late 1960s and 1970s, but as I conducted the oral histories that make up the backbone of this book, without exception every gay man painted a particularly bleak portrait of gay health care in that period.[3] Many dreaded that disclosure of their sexual activities would not remain confidential with their doctor, leading to ridicule from their families, termination from their jobs, or both, and these concerns had merit. One former client of a city-run VD clinic in Chicago remembered, "They weren't very nice . . . the help in that place, the clinic was just foul to gay people, just nasty."[4] Furthermore, venereal disease testing at Department of Health clinics in many cities commonly required disclosure of the patient's name and of all previous sexual partners before treatment was given. If a patient tested positive, the Department of Health systematically contacted each partner to inform him or her of

Figure 1. Nurse Wanda Lust with an inset of performer Stephen Jones. Photograph by Thousand Words Unlimited and from the collection of Gary Chichester.

the possible exposure to disease and to facilitate testing and treatment. While this process seems logical for disease containment, it served the opposite function, as many gay men, especially those who were not completely out of the closet, avoided testing because of the notification protocol. Whether because they did not want to deal with ignorant or homophobic staff members, make themselves and all of their sexual partners vulnerable to a very public coming out, or simply did not know the names of their sexual partners, gay

Figure 2. Nurse Wanda Lust visiting a patient with friends at Rush Presbyterian Hospital. Photograph by Thousand Words Unlimited and from the collection of Gary Chichester.

men often felt alienated from many city-run health clinics and from mainstream medicine writ large.

Compounding the problem of distrust of mainstream medicine within the gay community was a general ignorance of gay health issues among medical professionals. Until the 1970s, nearly all the medical literature and education on homosexuals focused on homosexuality itself as an illness in need of treatment.[5] As a result, doctors remained uninformed about how to diagnose and treat actual illnesses within the gay community, particularly those that manifested in slightly different ways than in the heterosexual population. Survey responses from doctors in 1978 showed that more than 84 percent of doctors believed they did not have adequate education in medical school to address these issues.[6] Consequently, sexually transmitted diseases among gay men often went undetected and untreated until in advanced stages.[7] Uneducated doctors could easily overlook gonorrhea symptoms in a gay man if the examination did not include a throat culture, a test not included in the standard examination for a heterosexual man. Unless a gay patient felt comfortable enough to inform his doctor of his sexual practices and the doctor knew the appropriate medical response, syphilis could go undetected and untreated.[8] By the end of the 1970s, some venereal diseases appeared much more frequently among gay men than in the general population.[9] Desperate for health care but with nowhere to turn gay men looked to one another for medical advice and treatment. A Chicago bathhouse owner became a sought out medical "expert" on how to perform reasonably reliable at-home tests for VD: "Milk the penis and if you get a white discharge, you probably got it."[10] The rare private doctor that neither price gouged nor violated patient confidentiality quickly became a local celebrity and was in high demand.

In response to these insufficient solutions, a colorful cast of doctors and activists built a largely self-sufficient gay medical system that challenged, collaborated with, and educated mainstream health practitioners. By decade's end, the health network included community clinics, outreach programs, national professional organizations, and a research infrastructure. Taking inspiration from the political health rhetoric employed by the Black Panther, feminist, and antiurban renewal movements and putting government funding to new and often unintended uses, gay health activists of the 1970s changed the medical and political understandings of sexuality and health to reflect the new realities of their own sexual revolution.

The history of this national gay health network challenges our understanding of gay politics in the 1960s, 1970s, and 1980s. The usual declension narrative, in which the leftist politics of the 1960s gives way to a rightward political shift, is insufficient for capturing both the creativity and the effectiveness of those gay health activists in the 1970s and 1980s who were determined to save lives and survive a changing political climate. LGBTQ activists did not tame their politics in the face of strengthening conservative opposition but rather adapted their tactics and political framing to affect change in the new political landscape.[11] From this perspective, the relationship between the state and homosexuality appears more nuanced, assimilating, and productive than a simple case of antagonism and oppression might suggest. Though historians have demonstrated the state's attempts to demand straightness from its citizens, this history of gay health activism suggests that the state can overlook, and at times even nurture, homosexuality as long as it also results in submission to state power.[12] In other words, the state in the 1970s cared less that there were gay citizens than that they left state systems and structures unchallenged.

Indeed, the gay health network that arose in this period grew directly out of Great Society programs. The links between gay health networks and the federal state grew stronger throughout the 1970s and set the stage for a strained relationship during the early AIDS crisis.[13]

Moreover, an examination of the roots of gay health clinics and their central activists brings the interdependence and complementary nature of various radical groups during this period into sharper focus.[14] Gay health activism, which began to emerge in the 1970s, had firm roots in the social movement politics of the late 1960s. Many gay health activists were veterans of these movements, and gay activists employed health as a political organizing tool in ways similar to many movements in the early 1970s. Gay health activism reflected the capitalist critiques of the antiwar and social medicine movements by incorporating free and sliding-scale fee structures in clinics. Building on the examples of the Black Panthers and Brown Berets, gay health activists learned to frame the struggle for health care as a form of political liberation by arguing that health disparities both exemplified and fueled discrimination. Gay health activists also embraced the idea of empowering individuals and communities to be their own health advocates and sources of information, much like feminist women's health movement activists. In many ways, gay health activists borrowed the best attributes of health activism occurring in other social movements and combined them as they built a national gay health network.

The analysis of these clinics brings clarity to how concepts of health factored into gay sexual and political culture, demonstrating in particular a much greater concern for sexual health in gay culture in the 1970s than previously depicted. Early AIDS literature, particularly fictionalized depictions of the early epidemic, often portrayed the preceding decade as a carefree decade-long orgy of sorts, paving the way for critiques that blamed "promiscuity" and personal irresponsibility for the early spread of the disease. The relatively meager literature on the gay liberation period has not yet erased this notion, or at least not with enough heft to change public perception of the decade. In fact, histories of gay liberation rightly claim newfound sexual freedom and decreased policing of homosexuality as defining attributes of the 1970s, but in doing so often inadvertently reinforce the portrayal of the decade as a sexual free-for-all with no concerns for sexual health. The work of these clinics and their relationships to the larger communities they served suggest that sexual health was often intertwined with gay liberation and the shifting gay sexual norms of the decade. In short, many men had a lot of sex with a lot of other men without the shame or harassment of previous decades, but they also got tested and treated for VD regularly and saw that as a necessary part of being sexually active. From this new vantage point, the early spread of AIDS becomes not about multiple partners or irresponsibility, but rather about a new disease with poorly understood modes of transmission. While I anticipated that many of these topics would surface in the course of my research, I was often surprised by the nuance my findings bring to the literature.

Though I desperately wanted to devote equal attention to the health activism of gay communities and lesbian communities, all sources showed that lesbians, though active in women's health and to a lesser extent gay health activism, worked far less on addressing lesbian-specific health concerns in the 1970s than their gay counterparts. Furthermore, the lesbian health activism that did exist was largely done within women's health clinics with little regard for, or communication with, gay health organizing. A focus on health issues specifically often exacerbated preexisting political (and biological) differences between gay men and lesbians during this decade so that they commonly approached health from different physical experiences and political frameworks. One gay and lesbian health guide from the 1980s attributed the segregation of gay health services from lesbian offerings, "in large part, [to] lesbian and gay men's health issues [being] radically different."[15] With the differences between gay and lesbian health activism far outweighing their similarities, a cohesive narrative arc that could move through time became extremely difficult to develop and maintain. Finally, because lesbian health activism around lesbian-specific health issues was relatively minor in this period, identifying and collecting archival sources that could sustain an equal study of gays and lesbians proved impossible. Here, then, I focus predominantly on gay health activism. Where possible, this history illuminates the difficult and complex relationship between gay men and lesbians in the 1970s, particularly when it came to issues of health and health services, as lesbians were at best left to fend for themselves, and at worst excluded entirely.

While the gay health network of the 1970s reorients our view of the relations between sexuality and the state and between various political movements, the individual clinics profiled in this study came to gay health from different local political contexts, and different activists propelled them. Over the course of the 1970s more than two dozen gay community health clinics came into existence, many of them lasting from only a few weeks to only a few years and leaving little historical evidence beyond ads scattered across local gay newspapers. Out of these many clinics, three case studies anchor *Before AIDS*: Fenway Community Health Clinic in Boston, the Gay Community Services Center in Los Angeles, and Howard Brown Memorial Clinic in Chicago. I interweave the stories of these three clinics with brief examples from other clinics around the country, examinations of individuals who were influential at multiple sites, and analyses of national networking among organizations. By focusing on these three cities and revealing them as the three major centers of gay health activism in the period before AIDS, I move beyond a historical narrative that centers on New York City and San Francisco.[16] These three clinics were trailblazers of gay health activism in the 1970s and the most influential, innovative, and lasting organizations of that period. By the early years of the AIDS crisis, when their volunteers, practitioners, and researchers became first responders to an epidemic whose treatment and epidemiology were not yet understood, these clinics had already solidified their significance to the gay and medical communities. They gained that significance and those reputations by navigating unique social and political terrains in ways that resonated with their local clients through ideology, organizational structure, and service offerings.

Activists determined to protect their neighborhood from redevelopment first started the Fenway Community Health Clinic in Boston as equal parts community-organizing effort and health service. The idea of opening a health clinic in the Fenway neighborhood came to two resident activists after the pair visited a newly opened Black Panther–operated health clinic that earned notoriety in the local press and fame among Boston activists.[17] That clinic, consisting of just a trailer, provided health services to the surrounding community and politically mobilized area residents. It also stood directly in the path of bulldozers slated to raze the neighborhood in preparation for the Inner Belt Road, or what would have been called I-695.[18] David Scondras, the director of community services at the Boston Center for Older Americans in the Fenway neighborhood, remembered that he saw the Black Panther Clinic as "an organizing tool to get everyday people who otherwise were not very political involved in the Black Panther Party. . . . It gave all of us an idea, which was that we should go out to the neighborhood and start organizing our community."[19] The political strategy behind the Black Panther Clinic resonated with the Fenway activists as developers and bulldozers from the Boston Redevelopment Authority also threatened their financially struggling neighborhood, having already demolished three hundred low-income housing units in 1968 and with plans to level more. Aware of both the political power of the Black Panther Clinic and the unmet medical needs of their own racially diverse and economically disadvantaged residents, Scondras and Linda Beane, a Northeastern University graduate nursing student, teamed up, using their complementary interests to open the renegade Fenway clinic in the Boston Center for Older Americans.[20] The clinic was one of many community-based organizations, including a food co-op, newspaper, and childcare, designed to make residents more politically engaged, unified, and organized to combat the state-approved developers attacking their neighborhood. Among its many health offerings and programs, the clinic offered gay-friendly VD testing.

In Los Angeles, a small group of gay men cast the gay health services they sought to offer in a different political light, that of gay survival of what they termed oppression sickness. Infusing gay liberation politics with the political rhetoric of many radical political movements in Los Angeles, veteran activists Don Kilhefner, Morris Kight, and John Platania understood the political, physical, mental, financial, and chemical struggles of gay community members as all symptoms of the same illness—oppression sickness. Oppression sickness was a broad concept that encapsulated any of the negative personal experiences that could be traced back to oppression or discrimination. The Gay Community Services Center Kilhefner, Kight, and Platania founded to address these symptoms and battle the larger societal illness of oppression offered a wide range of services from VD testing to support groups and from job training programs to drug rehabilitation. Oppression sickness infected the gay community, but these founders saw the larger society as the carrier of the disease and positioned the Gay Community Services Center as a service provider for the gay community as well as an idealistic catalyst for inoculating the larger society by fighting homophobia and structural forms of oppression. Each of the center's offerings placed gay identity and politics at its core. This political framing resonated with many local gay communities but had to be bridled and recast in order to garner the state funding and tax status the founders deemed imperative for the center's long-term success.

If Boston's clinic emerged out of a neighborhood threatened and Los Angeles' clinic grew from gay liberation politics applied to health disparities,

Chicago's Howard Brown Memorial Clinic can be traced back to gay doctors' frustration over incomplete medical training. As a medical student at the University of Chicago, David Ostrow realized that none of his medical training prepared him for the medical needs he saw in the gay bars and social gatherings he visited in his downtime. In response, he started a group to provide a supportive community for gay medical students who encountered homophobia in their classes and medical training. Ostrow envisioned that these medical students could offer emotional support to one another as well as academic and scientific collaboration as they sought to supplement their formal education by identifying and addressing the medical needs of the gay community. After an autumn 1973 ad in the *Gay Crusader*, the local gay newspaper, instructed those interested in joining the group to call, the rotary phone in Ostrow's small one-bedroom apartment rang off the hook.[21] Surprised, he found himself discussing with callers needs much more numerous and complicated than those of gay medical students simply needing social support. He realized that a large portion of the gay community, far larger than just gay medical students, was hungry for medical services and information. Ostrow described in an interview the scores of calls he received: "A third were from gay medical students . . . another equally large group of calls were people wanting to know where they could go to get good, respectful, nonjudgmental medical care for gay related health issues . . . and a third of these calls were from people who wanted to have sex with the gay medical students and they usually started out, 'Hello, are you a gay medical student?' and it went downhill from there."[22] As he took each call, answering questions in his native New Jersey accent, the need for gay health services became more and more apparent. Ostrow relayed the situation to other group members in meetings held at bars, businesses, and members' homes over the course of several weeks. As the long Chicago winter began to thaw into spring in 1974, the group began expanding their mission to include services beyond solely providing social support for medical students and professionals. By decade's end, the Howard Brown Memorial Clinic was the leading national research institution on gay health, serving thousands of clients annually through both in-clinic and outreach services.

Just as each of these clinics had a different political origin, they each presented their own research challenges. Boston proved the most difficult, as most of the organization's archives from the 1970s were discarded during a move to a new facility in the early 1980s. With only a thin file of organizational archives to work from, I took full advantage of the neighborhood newspaper, the *Fenway News*, as well as one of its founding editors, Stephen Brophy, to chart the history of the growing health clinic and identify the names of key figures in its development. I also contacted the existing Fenway Clinic, asking for any historical documents they still had as well as the names of any long-standing staff members. Fortunately, they had just commissioned a history of the organization and had contact information for a handful of clinic veterans from the 1970s willing to meet with me.[23] Combining these sources, I was able to piece together a fairly complete timeline of the clinic's development and conduct a dozen interviews (both on and off the record) that then pointed me to other sources, such as granting agencies and state records. In comparison, both Los Angeles and Chicago were far easier, as each clinic's records from the 1970s resided in community archives, though unprocessed when I went through them.[24] Even in their slightly jumbled state, these archives were extensive and made obvious the names of collaborative agencies and important figures that I pursued for interviews. I also sought out opportunities to present my research in public settings and would often have audience members come forward afterward with recollections or suggestions for additional sources. I then layered these individual clinic archives that I had compiled on top of deep readings of local newspapers, state archives, proceedings of medical and public health conferences, medical journals, and a broader national political context gleaned from national newspapers.

Interviews and individuals made this history possible to tell. I formally interviewed over twenty activists, doctors, and patients, most of them multiple times and over a series of years. The majority of these interviews were conducted in person in people's homes, offices, local coffee shops, or nearby parks, though some were via phone. They were difficult to set up, as many potential interview subjects were impossible to find after forty years, or they had passed away, many from AIDS. Some of those who remained saw their work in the clinics as tangential to their lives (then or now) and not worthy of my time or theirs despite my assurances to the contrary. Many argued that they hadn't really "done anything important." Another portion of those who refused to be interviewed suggested that the real story was AIDS or that the seriousness of AIDS made their contributions in the 1970s less significant. A handful refused to talk with me because the memories were too painful, as

AIDS had claimed so many of their friends or coworkers. Even though I asked specifically about events and issues that predated AIDS, the epidemic cast a shadow over all the interviews, resulting in much emotional labor for both the interview subjects and me as well as posing a real challenge in reconciling recollections with historical timelines. Thankfully, I quickly learned to come equipped with tissues and deploy the gay community press and newspapers that abound in each of these cities to spark memories and serve as cross-references. Those I interviewed often suggested others to interview, occasionally even providing contact information or introductions. For every person that agreed to be recorded and quoted, there were others who kindly refused while also sharing their memories in short introductory conversations. I sometimes used these informal interviews as opportunities to clarify an event or issue that I didn't fully understand or simply to get a better sense of the clinics. Many of those I interviewed, even those who did not want to be quoted or recorded, opened their basements, closets, and attics to reveal their personal records and ephemera from the clinics, sometimes simply handing them over to me. These dust-covered binders, boxes, envelopes, and folders contained much of the archival treasure that undergirds this book.

The 1970s offered a brief historical moment during which four major social and political factors converged to create and nurture gay health activism: gay liberation, the questioning of medical authority by various marginalized groups, the continuation of 1960s radicalism, and Great Society–era government policies that encouraged community health efforts. The confluence of these four forces allowed for gay health activism to take many forms in the period before the AIDS crisis, including community clinics, outreach programs, and research collaborations. Gay health activism in the 1980s responded to the AIDS crisis and a much more hostile fiscal and political environment by relying on and adding to the strong gay medical infrastructure laid by activists in the previous decade under much easier and more politically supportive circumstances.

The 1970s witnessed a militant shift in the political organizing of gay and lesbian communities that translated into proud declarations of homosexuality and an unprecedented number of services, commercial businesses, and organizations aimed at obtaining greater political power and rights for gays and lesbians. Many within gay communities point to the Stonewall riots of 1969, during which patrons of the Stonewall Inn in New York City's Greenwich

Village, many of whom were gender nonconforming people of color, retaliated against police attempting a raid, as the spark that set off the gay rights movement of the 1970s.[25] However, the history of gay communities and political activism suggests that the roots of gay liberation go back to the years immediately following World War II, when, prompted by the social and financial freedom and common single-sex environments of the war, homosexual men and women began to create communities and underground political organizations for themselves.[26] Starting in the 1950s, the Mattachine Society for men and the Daughters of Bilitis for women blazed the early trails for mounting a political response against the discrimination of homosexuals, or as they called themselves, homophiles. While the politics and tactics of these early groups were later deemed too tame and assimilationist by their radical successors, they were the first to mobilize homophile communities and create a national political network complete with newsletters, national conferences, and a political platform.[27] As the late 1960s became engulfed in social protests, political unrest, and sexual revolution, gay political activism began to shift toward a more militant and radical focus.[28] Starting in 1966 with the Compton Cafeteria riots in San Francisco and the Black Cat riots in Los Angeles, spontaneous and anger-filled protests, often by some of the most marginalized members of the community, began to replace the carefully planned and choreographed pickets of the homophile movement.[29] These protests and the emotions they represented came to epitomize gay politics in the 1970s as lesbians and gay men rejected their historical oppression, demanded political rights, and created social services and organizations to achieve their equality.[30] This zeitgeist and politics provided the political underpinning of gay health activism, the creation of gay community clinics, and the motivation for all the necessary volunteers. By the end of the 1970s, the radicalism at the heart of gay liberation had faded, giving way to a more commercial, assimilation-minded politics.[31] For the brief period of the 1970s, however, the politics and ethos of gay liberation proved invaluable to gay and lesbian health activists as they challenged mainstream medicine's long-standing identification of homosexuality as a physical and mental illness.[32]

Gay health activists represented just one of many groups that questioned medical authority during this period. A broad range of social and political movements of the late 1960s and early 1970s incorporated a critique of mainstream medicine and a demand for access to quality health care into their larger rhetoric and politics. The Black Panthers created a number of community health services to address a lack of access in poor, urban, black communities.[33] Women organized for quality reproductive care, with women of color fighting for protection from sterilization abuse, and middle-class, mostly white, women seeking access to abortion.[34] Disabled and institutionalized people also began to demand greater say in their treatment and autonomy.[35] The discovery of the Tuskegee Syphilis Experiment and the revelation about widespread Medicare and Medicaid fraud within the medical profession also encouraged the questioning of medical authority by marginalized groups during this period.[36]

Gay health activists demanded that the medical establishment change its pathological diagnosis of homosexuality to ease the social and political oppression of gay and lesbian patients. For almost a century leading up to the 1970s, doctors equated homosexuality with an illness that should be prevented, treated, and eradicated. By branding homosexuals as innately ill, doctors cemented their social and political marginalization and opened the door to various forms of "treatment" ranging from intensive therapy to electroshock treatments and experimental surgeries.[37] As a result of the work of gay health activists and gay liberationists, the 1970s witnessed a shift in the relationship between homosexuals and the medical profession, making it the first decade in which homosexuals were not classified as sick or diseased because of their sexuality. Through a combination of protests, gay men and lesbians coming out within the medical profession, and gay and lesbian community organizations offering their own health services, mainstream medicine began to divorce homosexuality from illness in the 1970s.[38] The successful action at the 1973 American Psychiatric Association annual meeting to have homosexuality officially removed from the *Diagnostic and Statistical Manual of Mental Disorders*, a list of symptoms and illnesses used to diagnose and treat mental illness, serves as perhaps the best-known example of these efforts.[39] Gays and lesbians employing the militancy of gay liberation and the larger attack on medical authority by numerous minority groups combined to challenge successfully the medical theories linking sexuality to illness. The AIDS epidemic in the 1980s posed a new challenge to decoupling homosexuality and illness among medical professionals and in society at large, as the disease was initially deemed a "gay plague."[40] However, the political ethos of the gay community and the mounting opposition to medical authority combined in the 1970s to create a period ripe for gay health activism and the renegotiation of the relationship between homosexuality and illness.

The political climate and government policies of the early 1970s also proved central to the birth and growth of gay health activism during this period. Many of the main actors in gay health began their political, and even medical, careers in the social and political movements of the late 1960s. As they focused their attention on gay health, their earlier experiences clearly informed the ways in which they organized gay health institutions and services. In Boston, former antiwar activists used the protest and community-organizing tactics learned in that movement to create a community health clinic as a means to save their neighborhood from gentrification and redevelopment. In Los Angeles, gay liberationists used their limited access to quality and affordable care as an example of their larger political oppression, borrowing directly from the Black Power and women's movements of the period.

Equally important to the political mind-set of individual activists were the government policies and national political conversations of the late 1960s and early 1970s. The Great Society programs that made up much of President Johnson's domestic policy in the 1960s not only set the stage for gay health activism in the 1970s through funding and public health initiatives but also provided insight into some of the important debates and concerns of the post–World War II period.[41] Johnson faced a health crisis created by rising medical costs, growing dependence on employment-based medical insurance, and a shrinking number of medical professionals. In the 1960s, an increasing number of people, often those with the greatest need for medical care, experienced a decrease in their access to quality and affordable medical care. In response, Johnson employed an approach that had been effective in addressing many of the issues that grew out of the nation's high poverty rates: community-based programs. Great Society policies placed individual communities at the center of government programs, allowing for federal monies to support services that were often designed by local community members to address the specific problems they faced.[42] These policy initiatives informed the development of gay health activism in two ways. First, they created a mind-set within struggling communities that community members could create solutions to their problems and that the government would help. Second, and more practically, Great Society programs encouraged the creation of community health clinics for underserved communities through direct funding and fund-matching programs.

In this context, state initiatives actually provided, albeit unintentionally, for gay and lesbian health activism.

Against this larger backdrop, *Before AIDS* makes five central claims, with one chapter dedicated to each. First, gay liberation emanated from distinctly local circumstances and is better understood as local gay activism happening in multiple locations across the country rather than as a unified national movement. Second, and relatedly, gay health activism emerged from a wide variety of 1960s social and political movements, such as feminism, antipoverty programs, and civil rights activism, and often reflected a local political context more than any national gay political agenda. From these two perspectives, gay liberation is one among many contributing factors in the development of gay services and institutions, rather than the sole impetus. Third, despite the continued marginalization of gays in U.S. society during the period, the state actually contributed significantly, though often unintentionally, to the health activism of gay men in the 1970s. This occurred through funding and policy making that led indirectly to the founding and evolution of gay community health clinics throughout the decade. Fourth, as a consequence of community clinics, outreach programs, and research efforts, the meanings of sexuality and health within both gay political and mainstream medical communities changed significantly over the course of the 1970s. Finally, a substantial and multifaceted gay medical infrastructure predated the AIDS crisis of the 1980s, a fact that is, with few exceptions, overlooked in the vast literature on AIDS (not to mention my initial daydreamed history of gay community health clinics). This existing infrastructure made significant contributions to gay health and mainstream medicine in the 1970s and was well positioned to serve effectively on the frontlines of the early AIDS epidemic of the 1980s.

CHAPTER 1

REIMAGINING GAY LIBERATION

Arising in the late 1960s, gay liberation sparked the exponential growth of gay institutions and services, including those for health. As a movement, gay liberation championed and personified a militant gay and lesbian politics that redirected the blame for homosexual oppression to society rather than to homosexuals themselves and celebrated gay and lesbian sexuality. Taking advantage of diminished policing of gay spaces and a larger political context that challenged the status quo, gay liberation embraced the concept of "gay is good," a complete shift from earlier political and medical framings of homosexuality. The movement also witnessed the proliferation of businesses, newspapers, and social outlets by and for gay communities in cities across the country. Nevertheless, it was local politics, activists, and contexts that directed the evolution of these services and institutions more than any national gay liberation movement or politics. Indeed, the gay health activism of the 1970s demonstrates that gay liberation played, at times, only a minor role in the development of gay health services and the resulting gay institutions.

Among gay health activists and in the clinics they started, gay liberation rarely conformed to the imagined history common in today's LGBTQ communities, which homogenizes and romanticizes 1970s gay experiences by suggesting that gay urban communities across the country acted similarly, held shared beliefs, and deployed common tactics to fight the same battles. Gay liberation as a cultural and political movement mattered as gay communities began to take on new shapes and meanings in the 1970s, and gay health activism does not discount its significance. The history of gay health activism, however, demands a reimagining of gay liberation, replacing the national movement with local examples of vaguely similar rhetoric sculpted by local contexts. This new vantage point provides a richer and more accurate understanding of the meanings of gay liberation while also revealing that many organizations and services that came to epitomize gay liberation were only gay through circumstance.

"Already Part of the We"

In Boston, gay liberation appears as only a tangential factor in the Fenway clinic's origins and early growth. Rather, it was locally oriented opposition to gentrification that unified the neighborhood and propelled its activism. After the city approved the Boston Redevelopment Authority's Fenway Urban Renewal Project in 1965 and began razing portions of the neighborhood in late 1967, local residents created a wide array of social services to unify the community and resist the Redevelopment Authority's plan.[1] Along with a food co-op, a newspaper, a childcare center, and a community playground, a small clinic emerged as yet another form of resistance through community building. The thinking behind these enterprises was simple: if the Boston Redevelopment Authority wanted to redevelop the neighborhood through razing, residents sought to revitalize the neighborhood themselves, eliminating the need to raze. They took advantage of federal funding through Great Society programs and deftly used photo opportunities and political optics to make destroying the neighborhood unsavory for local politicians. Thus, on a summer evening in 1971, the first in a long line of Fenway residents in need of medical care arrived at the Boston Center for Older Americans, a senior drop-in center located on the neighborhood's eastern edge operated by the First Church of Christ, Scientist. Clinic cofounder David Scondras had decided to use the center's space for an after-hours community clinic despite the Christian Science church's teachings that members should maintain their physical and mental health through the use of prayer rather than medicine. Unbeknownst to center management or church officials and with the Black Panther Clinic as a model, Scondras, with the help of nursing graduate student and Fenway resident Linda Beane, began offering health services to Fenway residents, including gay-friendly VD testing to the resident gay community.[2]

Scondras, a recent Harvard graduate, antiwar activist, and computer pro-

grammer, had come to live in the neighborhood while working as an econom-
ics instructor at Northeastern University on the neighborhood's eastern
border. In the Fenway, he continued his work in the antiwar movement that
had begun at Harvard and took the job at the Center for Older Americans as
a way to get to know neighborhood residents. At Northeastern, the young
instructor and political activist with a bushy black beard befriended Beane,
who led a student group that was dedicated to the community health movement and provided free medical care. A fellow Fenway resident and also a
veteran of the antiwar movement, Beane applied her political acumen to
neighborhood issues, including organizing Fenway residents at the area's
Westland Avenue Community Center.[3]

Tensions with the Church of Christ, Scientist and the rapidly increasing
number of patients made it impossible for the Fenway clinic to operate out of
the Boston Center for Older Americans for long. As a result, in early 1973, the
group found and rented the basement of a small building, "a defunct antique
shop," with an alleyway entrance off Haviland Street in the heart of the Fenway
neighborhood, to house a new community clinic.[4] The basement on Haviland
Street was a far cry from a clinic at the time Scondras rented it. As one activist
reminisced in an interview, "They got my brother-in-law to be their pro-bono
lawyer who got them their lease for a dollar a year."[5] Community members
cleaned and painted the abandoned basement and constructed makeshift
exam rooms, a filing area, a waiting room, and a lab. One remembered, "I
helped with some of the physical stuff when they were building, putting some
of the flooring down and things like that, which was all done by probably
some people who knew what they were doing and most people who didn't and
were just helping."[6] They furnished the clinic with a hodgepodge of secondhand and donated furniture, including seats from a defunct movie theater on
Boylston Street that served as waiting room chairs and medical equipment
from a retired Back Bay doctor, and opened the clinic's doors to the community in August 1973.[7] Medical supplies were often "acquired" by volunteers
who were also physician's assistants, nurses, doctors, or medical students dedicated to providing free health care. A longtime volunteer physician at the
Fenway clinic remembered, "I'd filch stuff from the hospital and bring it over."[8]
Nearly everything in the clinic was borrowed, used, or homemade, but from
its opening, it was busy serving the Fenway residents who oftentimes had
limited or no access to other health care.

Figure 3. The initial main entrance to the Fenway Community Health Center was in an alleyway off a side street in the heart of the Fenway neighborhood. Fenway Community Health Center records, 1972–2007, M172, box 10, folder 27, Northeastern University Archives, Boston.

Far from being focused on the gay population, the Fenway Community Health Clinic, both in its nascent stage at the Boston Center for Older Americans and in its first official home in the basement on Haviland, reflected and served, according to its patient demographics, the diverse neighborhood residents. A third of the Fenway population lived below the poverty level, scraping by with a median annual income of $2,027.[9] One reporter writing in 1977 described the area as a "low-income, low-rent neighborhood, its population of 4,000 is somewhat transient, consisting mainly of students, welfare families, young working people, and elderly people. It has long had a reputation for street crime, drugs, and prostitution and was once one of Boston's more notorious red-light districts."[10] In a city infamous for its racial segregation and tension during the 1970s, the Fenway was a rare example of integration of not only blacks and whites but also a considerable immigrant, mostly Latino, population. Responding to the neighborhood's needs, the clinic treated almost all nonemergency medical issues, from child immunizations, blood pressure tests, and the flu to testing and treating VD, pre- and postoperative care for most surgeries, and gynecological services.[11] A longtime volunteer physician described the clinic services as a "basically primary care model. If you had high blood pressure, you'd come in. If you had diabetes, you'd come in. If you needed an annual physical, you'd come in."[12] While at the Boston Center for Older Americans, the clinic served a small but diverse population that included the elderly, women, children, and gays.[13] After the move to the Haviland basement in 1973, there was more physical space and more volunteers to reach out to each of these groups specifically. In addition to its regular daytime operating hours, during which anyone could schedule an appointment or drop by, the clinic opened its doors to specific populations in the evening and on weekends, including a gay health clinic on Wednesday nights.[14] The clinic's services and outreach to these specific populations reflected the diversity of the neighborhood and illuminated the deficiencies in the existing health-care system of the early 1970s. However, gay liberation rhetoric and politics were just a faint background hum to the neighborhood's chants against gentrification and for access to affordable quality health care.

Clinic board meetings, which were intended to include and galvanize the entire community, looked more like town hall meetings and easily lasted several hours, which undoubtedly made them inaccessible for some in the community with limited time.[15] One resident described how meetings would last "anywhere from three to five hours; yeah, they were long. Most of us on the board with some exceptions didn't have experience in health care, or the management of clinics or human resources . . . we were the blind leading the blind."[16] In the early years, anyone who was associated with the clinic (founders, volunteers, patients, or even just neighbors) was welcome to attend the meetings, create agenda items on the spot, engage in debate, and vote on any and all decisions.[17] This democratic structure reflected the political approach of many young, New Left–affiliated organizations of the period and was meant to foster personal investment in the clinic and larger Fenway community in the face of the encroaching redevelopment.

The way in which services specifically for gay patients became established within this very open structure illuminates how indirectly gay liberation influenced the Fenway clinic and the tight-knit community it served. With the clinic's dedication to serving the entire Fenway community (of which gay men were a small part), creating and maintaining a gay health collective to formalize the clinic's already established treatment of gay men was relatively easy. A doctor at Boston's Homophile Community Health Center, which provided gay-friendly counseling to gays from around the city, asked clinic cofounder David Scondras if the Fenway clinic could provide medical backup to his patients. Taking advantage of the open, town hall–style board meetings, Scondras pitched the idea in April 1974 and received a warm reception. The Gay Health Collective of the Fenway Community Health Clinic began offering Wednesday night sessions on May 22, 1974.

Neither the inclusion of gay services at the Fenway clinic nor their formalization in the Gay Health Collective's weekly sessions should be mistaken for gay liberation activism. While a handful of the Fenway activists were gay, Scondras among them, few were explicitly out or active in gay liberation organizations, focusing instead on the antiwar movement or the struggle with the Boston Redevelopment Authority. In fact, those who had insisted on the inclusion of gay health services at the clinic's founding were often not out to one another or the Fenway clinic community. According to Scondras, "It was sort of an unspoken thing. No one ever got up and said, 'Hey, I'm gay.'"[18] Shedding more light on the political affiliations of the Fenway clinic during this period, one activist recalled, "It never really became a gay anything, it was just a place where gay people came . . . you advocated for anybody who needed help . . . we never thought of ourselves as gay, straight, white, black."[19] From this vantage point, Fenway residents never thought the Fenway Community Health Clinic directly related to gay liberation, and neither did the clinic itself. Rather, the clinic was an embodiment of progressive New Left politics, including the antiwar, antigentrification, labor, hippie, women's, student, and civil rights movements, which challenged oppression in all forms, including homophobia. The clinic and many of its activists appear as gay allies rather than as actually gay. In this way, the New Left political and cultural milieu appears a better political point of origin for the Fenway clinic than gay liberation. However, the existence and success of gay health services at the Fenway Community Health Clinic from its inception did make the clinic unique.

While Scondras, who couldn't remember ever specifically disclosing his own gay identity to the Fenway clinic community, was central in creating the Gay Health Collective, Ron Vachon was, perhaps more than anyone, the "gay face" of the clinic.[20] Vachon was "the backbone of the thing . . . big, tall, strong, French Canadian, very gentle, but six foot three, bearded, probably could have been a professional wrestler if he didn't go into medicine. He was working full-time at the Fenway clinic as a physician's assistant and was gay."[21] While finishing up his degree as a physician's assistant at Northeastern University in 1975, Vachon literally "wandered into the Wednesday night clinic for the first time because the man he was dating came in to pick up some files. There, he met then-medical director Sandy Reder, who on learning that Vachon was a physician's assistant, put him to work on the spot. Vachon stayed to become part of the collective, and ultimately, the center's first paid staff person."[22] He quickly became a leader at the clinic, even being considered for the position of executive director in the late 1970s, and always making sure that the clinic considered and met the medical needs of the gay community.[23] In short, because they "were already part of the we," already part of the Fenway community, a few activists who were gay were able to use the clinic's organizational structure and mission to shape the services of the clinic and meet the medical needs of the gay community specifically without appearing to be outspoken gay activists.[24] Gay health services originated at Fenway as part of the clinic's community health activism, not because of any specific gay organizing. In this way, both the activists and the clinic itself have a very different relationship with the closet—they were more in the closet or at least downplaying their gay affiliations—than appears typical in the existing history of out and proudly vocal gay institutions of this period.

Boston's gay population welcomed the opening of the Gay Health Collective at the Fenway for a number of reasons. First and foremost, it offered the only local, free, gay-friendly health services, which allowed gay men to avoid the ridicule they faced in many public clinics, the price gouging that was common in private doctors' offices, and the inherent risks of using medical insurance.[25] Moreover, the clinic was within less than a five-minute walk from the eastern border of the Fens cruising grounds, which made it an ideal location for gay men to stop in and get tested on their way either to or from the park. A volunteer doctor of the Gay Health Collective, himself a gay man, described his patients as "college kids, young adults, the bartenders . . . just the panoply of gay people as gay people were defined in the 70s. There definitely would be a mix of a stockbroker or lawyer, but not so many."[26] Another volunteer remembered, "I think we were caught off guard by the deluge of students and young folks that came for sexually transmitted diseases."[27] Word of the Fenway clinic's gay-friendly services quickly spread throughout the city's gay population via word of mouth, flyers in bars, and ads in *Gay Community News*. Shortly after its opening, the Wednesday night Gay Health Collective saw gay patients from all across the city and region. The clinic and its staff viewed and presented its gay services as a subsidiary to the larger mission of serving the neighborhood and providing low-cost, high-quality care, allowing it to remain a strong gay ally, but not actually gay. Regardless, it secured the Fenway clinic's position as a new Boston gay institution among the city's gay community.

VD screening and treatment for gay men began as one of nearly a dozen other programs run out of the clinic, aiding gay residents and quickly drawing gay clients from across the region. While the clinic quickly earned a reputation within the gay community as *the* gay clinic in town, it saw its services for gay clients as just another small piece of its offerings and distanced itself from close association with gay liberation or gay identity. A dozen years later, the clinic found itself on the frontlines of the AIDS crisis, on the cutting edge of gay and lesbian health services and research, and welcoming doctors and scientists from Harvard and the Centers for Disease Control in search of expert advice. While the Fenway clinic's legacy grew from its relationship to gay and lesbian health, that relationship took nearly a decade to truly blossom, and its roots originate in the wreckage of the eastern Fenway and the resultant anti-gentrification activism.

Front and Center

While gay liberation rhetoric and politics factored minimally in the creation of Boston's Fenway Community Health Clinic, they proved a driving, and politically radical, force in Los Angeles. In November 1969, the recently formed Los Angeles Gay Liberation Front (GLF) sublet a small office at one of the major intersections on the Silver Lake neighborhood's western border, a space that had most recently served as area headquarters for the Peace and Freedom Party in the local political elections, for which a GLF activist had volunteered.[28] The GLF sought to revolutionize society's sexual norms through many forms of activism as well as through gay community building. The office served as a drop-in center and meeting place for gay liberationists, but also, in the smaller of its two rooms, housed a gay helpline. As the Los Angeles GLF was, in late 1969 and early 1970, one of only a handful of telephone listings in the country with the word "gay" in its name, it became a lifeline of sorts for gay people across the country. On most nights, volunteer Don Kilhefner sat in his sleeping bag in the small back room with the phone receiver pressed against his ear. He later recalled, "Starting around eleven o'clock/eleven thirty the calls would come in from [the East Coast] and just roll across the country by time zone so that by about two or three o'clock in the morning I was putting down the phone and getting some sleep. I listened for a year, thirteen months, to these calls. 'I have an alcohol problem, I have a drug problem, I lost my job because I'm gay' . . . from A to Z, there they were, every night."[29] With every call, Kilhefner saw the relationship between the oppression of gay people and "sickness" grow stronger, as their oppression resulted in physical, mental, and financial problems.

In response to the growing list of gay issues illuminated by helpline callers and reflecting the political ethos and rhetoric of gay liberation in Los Angeles, Kilhefner formed the Gay Survival Committee, along with longtime activist Morris Kight, gay antiwar and union activist John Platania, and a handful of other GLF members who lived in Kilhefner's housing co-op. Platania later recorded his thoughts on the extent to which the issue of survival permeated the gay community at the time:

> Along with all the excitement, the activity, and celebration, we also began to see, see deeply, the kind of real human need that was in our community: the starvation, literally, the homelessness, the drugs, the alcohol, the disease. You know the plague is not new. It is not a stranger to the gay community. We have been dying for years of sexually trans- mitted diseases! For years and years before AIDS! We were dying of alcoholism and hepatitis before that. . . . There were no services; that's the point.[30]

During meetings of the Gay Survival Committee, Kilhefner, Kight, and Plata- nia first theorized about the link between sexual oppression and gay health. They coined the term "oppression sickness" to better understand how the problems of the gay community were rooted in its oppression and to explore the ways in which homophobia literally made gay people sick.[31] Oppression sickness encompassed physical, mental, financial, and political issues and

ailments common in the gay community—issues like job loss, violence, de-
pression, substance abuse, isolation, homelessness, medical malpractice, and
self-destructive behavior. The oppression sickness concept pushed beyond the
rigid boundaries of a medical understanding of health and illness and expanded gay liberation rhetoric to new terrain, blurring the lines between medical issues and political ones. From this perspective, fighting and curing
oppression sickness would demand more than political lobbying and protest
or doctor's visits and medication. Rather, the gay community would have to
mobilize on many fronts, provide numerous services, and address the larger
systemic and societal problems contributing to their oppression.

Because oppression sickness included nearly every outgrowth of oppression gay people encountered, members of the Gay Survival Committee
thought the most effective solution was to create a large social service organization that addressed all of these issues. The center would have programs attacking oppression sickness in every form possible: legal services for gay
service members who had been dishonorably discharged because of their
sexuality, pen pals for incarcerated gays who faced violence and injustice
within prisons, employment training and placement for gays who were fired
or who fled their oppression in school, numerous discussion and rap groups
on coming out and raising political awareness, dances, temporary housing,
substance abuse services, and a medical clinic, to name only a few programs.[32]
The range of services reflected the idealism and political commitment to radical gay liberation that shaped the Los Angeles political landscape. The site of
the Watts uprising, home to a strong Black Panther, Brown Beret, and radical
feminist contingent, Los Angeles provided a backdrop for a wide array of
radical leftist politics in the late 1960s and early 1970s. In addition, Los Angeles had already had a long tradition of being on the cutting edge of gay political activism, whether as the founding site for the Mattachine Society of the
early 1950s or as the location of the Black Cat riots of 1967. Inspired and fueled by the political activism and liberation discourse boiling over at the local
level, the concept of oppression sickness proved captivating. With the help of
John Platania, who at the time was a grant writer for a local nonprofit agency,
by the spring of 1971 the countless discussions of "oppression sickness" cul-
minated in a proposal of more than thirty pages, outlining needed services,
management hierarchies, organizational charts, and a preliminary budget for
a gay community services center.[33]

A center of this size and magnitude would draw on a deep local well of gay liberation activism but would also require access to public funding and political support. Consequently, the proposed structure of the organization sought to strike a delicate balance between remaining true to the organizers' radical politics and gaining support from the state. The resulting proposed organizational structure thus included positions common among professional nonprofits, such as an executive director, board members, and department managers. As Kilhefner recalled,

> We wanted [the center] to look like nothing [funders or government officials] could challenge. We were the revolutionaries. We were the radicals. We were the people quoting Che and Mao. They did not expect that from us. We made a conscious decision that this would not be a consensus group. It would not be run like the Gay Liberation Front, where every month we elected a different leader and decisions were made by consensus. This was an organization with hierarchy, with defined positions, just like . . . the Red Cross.[34]

This hierarchical organizational structure did, in many ways, clash with the political beliefs and practices of many of the contemporary gay and lesbian groups in Los Angeles. The GLF's gay community center came directly out of a local political movement that not only questioned heterosexist society but regularly used the rhetoric of political and social revolution to create a defiant and celebratory gay community.[35] As one handout proclaimed, the Gay Community Services Center "is making it possible for heretofore largely powerless people to mobilize the power necessary to change our own lives, and, growing out of this, the larger society in which we live."[36] In short, the Gay Survival Committee was attempting to attract funds and political support from the very society it sought to challenge, not unlike the Fenway community's use of federal funds to thwart city plans to demolish their neighborhood.

Despite the community center's conventional structure, the oppression sickness it sought to address resonated with the radical gay liberation rhetoric and politics in Los Angeles. The center would provide a place from which the gay community could attack its oppression and the larger oppressive society from many angles, while simultaneously creating a politically, physically, and mentally healthier community.[37] Armed with the lengthy proposal and the enthusiasm of other GLF members, Kilhefner and Kight rented a rickety old Victorian house at 1614 Wilshire Boulevard and formally opened the Los Angeles Gay Community Services Center in the fall of 1971.[38] In keeping with their vision of the organization, the men immediately began the incorporation and tax-exemption processes, which lasted over a year.[39] At the same time, they remained dedicated to their radical politics by placing themselves at the forefront of public protests and actions. In describing the politics of the center once it opened and the fervor of its volunteers and patrons, Kilhefner reminisced, "We had picket signs, must have had one hundred picket signs, almost for any occasion. So somebody would call and [report instances of homophobia] and within twenty-four hours we'd have picket signs . . . picketing. We were fighting back fast and instantly because this was movement building for us, community building for us, consciousness raising for us."[40] The Los Angeles Gay Community Services Center thus navigated the difficult path of being relevant to and worthy of support from two opposing political bodies, the state and the radical gay community. It was this combination that gave the center its distinctive character.

Beyond its emphasis on gay liberation, the birth and evolution of the Los Angeles Gay Community Services Center also reflects the strong radical political tradition of Los Angeles itself. In the decades immediately preceding the founding of the center, Los Angeles was a hotbed for the leftist and communist popular front and proved fertile ground for a number of radical organizations, including the Mattachine Society, the first national political organization for "homophiles" that emanated out of Los Angeles in the early 1950s.[41] Starkly different from the political culture of Boston, the Los Angeles radical political tradition primed both the city and activists for the work and vision of the Los Angeles Gay Community Services Center.

A focus on health was central to the Los Angeles Gay Community Services Center's success in gaining political and financial support from both the state and the gay community, just as it had been for the Fenway Community Health Clinic of Boston. Among center activists and patrons, health embodied a wide range of issues that went far beyond physical illnesses and spoke to a larger political oppression. The state, on the other hand, had a very limited notion of health wherein statistics on disease contacts and treatments carried much more weight than talk of political oppression.[42] The Gay VD Clinic was one of the few services within the Gay Community Services Center in which these

Gay Community Services Center
1614 West Wilshire Blvd.
Los Angeles, Calif.

Figure 4. The first Los Angeles Gay Community Services Center building was an old Victorian home in the Silver Lake neighborhood of Los Angeles. Los Angeles Gay Community Services Center, "Gay Community Services Center Brochure," box 3, folder 34, L.A. Gay & Lesbian Center Records, Coll2007-010, ONE National Gay & Lesbian Archives, USC Libraries, University of Southern California.

two understandings of health overlapped.[43] The clinic consisted of a series of three rooms. The first was a small room on the first floor in which people could wait, and nurses could conduct intake exams. The second was literally a closet that volunteers had converted, by removing its door and installing a light, into a laboratory for drawing blood and taking swabs. The third room was a screened-in porch with sheets hung up to provide privacy for exams.

Despite its ramshackle appearance, the clinic passed inspection in October 1972 and immediately began offering services.[44]

Dr. Ben Teller, an independently wealthy "hippie doctor" who had just moved back to the United States after working with the Centers for Disease Control in West Africa, served as the main point person for the clinic's development and subsequent operation.[45] At the request of Kilhefner and Kight, Teller agreed to share his license and liability insurance with the center and was given free rein to build the VD clinic as he saw fit. He recounted his vision in an interview:

> It would be a free clinic . . . run on donations . . . where gay people [men] could come and feel totally comfortable talking about their sexuality and . . . sexually transmitted diseases. They didn't have to have any shame or reservation explaining what was going on. . . . The waiting room would be filled with literature that would be relevant to them . . . it would be a place where professionals and paraprofessionals as well as patients could be totally open and honest about themselves and therefore promote good gay health. . . . That was the vision.[46]

Upon opening in the fall of 1972, the clinic came to embody much of Teller's vision. The clinic was furnished with a "hodgepodge" of mostly thrift store purchases from the local Goodwill with a few high-quality pieces that had been donated by a wealthy contributor.[47] Licensed gay doctors, nurses, and lab technicians volunteered to staff the clinic, which was entirely volunteer-run for the first few years.[48] Teller offered, "The effect [of being able to work in an openly gay environment] on the professionals was I think as great as it was on the patients." The willingness of everyone to work for free "testifies to the fact that the professionals were getting something out of it."[49]

The politics of the clinic were the same as the rest of the programs housed in the Gay Community Services Center—the Gay VD Clinic was designed to challenge an oppressive heterocentric society. Teller explained that opening the clinic was "a political statement that there was a need for this and it could be easily understood."[50] In addition to challenging a heterosexist society and ignorant mainstream medical establishment, the clinic also fostered gay community building, both among volunteers and patients. The walls were covered in posters depicting two gay men in a variety of positions that read "Don't

Give Him Anything but Love," and informational pamphlets covered the waiting-room tables.[51] Signs that Teller hung prominently around the clinic pleaded, "This clinic runs on love and money, please give some of both." He reminisced, "It was very much hippie and inspired, Gay Liberation Front inspired, hippie, I would say leftists, chaotic."[52]

Despite the expense to the early radical ideal of critiquing the state, the center's founders argued that, in order to provide the services the community needed, government funding was essential. Local, state, and federal grants allowed the entire center to grow, even though it funded relatively few of the center's expanding program offerings. Services like the men's VD program, the handful of alcohol and drug programs, and the interim housing program that obtained and maintained government (municipal, state, and federal) funding also brought in the most donations from community members.[53] Thus, while government funds benefited only a small number of programs, the donation revenue those programs generated was then shared among all the center's programs. The many rap groups and social events offered by the center required little in the way of funding, and many survived solely on the amounts allocated from the general donation funds.[54] As a result of the center's many programs, it quickly became, according to one person involved, "a very, very active place. . . . I remember being in their big living room with at least one hundred people in there at any one time in the different rooms."[55]

Government funding allowed existing offerings to grow in size, strength, and quality. Within a few short years, the center outgrew the dilapidated mansion on Wilshire Boulevard, moving in 1975 to a new and larger location at 1213 North Highland in the gay neighborhood of West Hollywood.[56] By 1978, the center provided services to 13,600 people per month and obtained roughly $750,000 in government funding. The funds came from many government sources, ranging from local to federal, including the Greater Los Angeles Area Community Action Agency, the Los Angeles County Department of Urban Affairs, the United States Department of Health, the Los Angeles Regional Family Planning Council, and the Comprehensive Employment and Training Act. [57] Part of the center's success reflected its greater access to local funding through Los Angeles County than other gay clinic counterparts in other cities, but its intentional design as an organization that would be palatable and attractive to government funding at all levels was an even more important factor.

In achieving their objective of becoming a strong institution that provided a wide array of social services to Los Angeles gays and lesbians, the center's founders were well served by their choice to seek and accept state funding. By 1976, the center consisted of three buildings: one for a temporary residential program for gay parolees, another for the center's residential rehabilitation program, and the third housing the actual center. In addition, the center offered a wide and growing set of more than two dozen services ranging from health clinics to rap groups to job training and placement programs to a secondhand store.[58] In 1975 the center served over one thousand people. Patron demographics show that the center attracted people of nearly every age and race with roughly 40 percent of service recipients being female.[59] By 1978, the men's VD clinic alone accounted for more than fifteen thousand visits annually to the center.[60]

The center's combination of radical politics and conventional structure proved a potent political elixir for Los Angeles because of the local political meanings and tactics associated with gay liberation. Bolstered by a radical, robust, and preexisting politics, the Los Angeles Gay Community Services Center not only emanated directly from gay liberation but also embodied the local definition and tactics of gay liberation—to radically overhaul societal sexual norms through a wide variety of protests, services, and personal interactions to destigmatize homosexuality. This political framing would not have translated well to other places because it was either too gay or too radical, illustrating the importance of local context in understanding gay liberation as a political movement and rhetoric.

Tandem Activism

Neither background nor primary force, gay liberation factored into the development of gay health services in Chicago as a social and personal awakening rather than as the larger political movement characteristic of Los Angeles. In 1965, David Ostrow began attending the University of Chicago as a sixteen year old with little interest in political activism and an internal struggle with his homosexuality, which he described as "something to be overcome in myself . . . it wasn't natural."[61] Upon arriving in the city's South Side Hyde Park neighborhood, Ostrow pursued not only his bachelor's degree but also set out on an academic path leading to an MD as well as a PhD in biochemistry. In the wake of a failed two-year marriage to his high school girlfriend, Ostrow, then immersed in his medical school training, finally came to terms with the sexual attraction to men he had felt since early adolescence, coming out as a gay man in 1972.[62] In his limited spare time, he began to explore Chicago's growing gay geography, visiting bars and bathhouses in the city's near and far north neighborhoods. In these gay businesses, he found a surprising number of other area medical students representing many different medical colleges who often complained that "a lot of what was taught to us in medical school was either homophobic or was ignorant. So, a bunch of us said . . . let's form a social organization to support us."[63] Thus, a gay medical students group was born. The formation of the group was in many ways typical of the period's zeitgeist, in terms of both student activism and a vibrant and growing gay community in Chicago. Ostrow recalled, "It's what everybody [did]. . . . You fe[lt] isolated from other people with whom you share[d] an interest and you fe[lt] left out at your job or school or something and you form[ed] a . . . group."[64]

Equal parts social and professional support, the group quickly moved from simply supporting gay medical students to also addressing the health needs of gay patients. As they set their sights on offering accurate, nonjudgmental, low-cost, and gay-friendly services, the gay medical students group had only a vague understanding of the tremendous need in the gay community and all that offering health services required. Ostrow recalled, "We had no idea of how we were going to do it."[65] The driving force behind their goals for gay health was a deep commitment to and love of medicine, rather than a political ethos, as in Los Angeles and Boston. For many members of the gay medical students group, medicine was not simply a career path or job, but a lifelong dream that, as they finished medical school, was becoming real. For those group members who went on to be central gay health activists in Chicago, a love of medicine, research, and science propelled them. In this way, gay health activism in Chicago combined both a passion for medicine and gay liberation symbiotically.

Among their initial efforts, the gay medical students group began educating area doctors and public health officials about how to better treat and engage the gay community—a decidedly different approach than the pickets and protests in Los Angeles. They created fact sheets, a very early and primitive version of the safe sex handbooks that would become common in the 1980s, which they sent to private doctors, city clinics, and gay men who called the group's phone number asking for more information.[66] Through these fact sheets and a few speaking engagements they arranged at local medical schools, city clinics, and professional development meetings, other organizations and gay community members learned of the group, adding to its ranks and reputation as an advocate for gay people in medicine. By the spring of 1974, as the group began to explore offering medical services to the gay community, nurses, medical technicians, and older and well-established medical professionals had eagerly joined the group. One such doctor was Dr. Stanley Wissner, who offered that the gay medical students could provide services under his medical license and malpractice insurance if they could find a space for a clinic.

In May 1974, a gay social service organization in Chicago, Gay Horizons, offered the group the space they needed to expand their services to include testing and treatment. At that time, Gay Horizons was a relatively small and new nonprofit organization with big plans for expansion. At the start of 1974, it consisted of a one-night-per-week coffeehouse, a collaborative program with the local gay teachers association to help gays and lesbians earn their GED, and a weekly business meeting open to the community.[67] Despite its relatively meager service offerings at the time, the mission and vision of Gay Horizons put the organization on a trajectory toward growth and a wide range of programs similar to the Los Angeles Gay Community Services Center, complete with "a Community Center and a professional Counseling Service."[68] The stated purpose of the organization, "to promote understanding and healthy development through assistance to . . . Gay people in bringing about an awareness of themselves as human beings and acceptance of their individual lifestyles, and an upgrading in the quality of their lives through the active promotion and support of specific programs to meet educational, emotional and social needs," complemented the aims of the gay medical students group in wanting to improve health care and education in the gay community.[69] While Gay Horizons and the medical students group were mutually beneficial for one another, they also had very different interests and methods. Gay Horizons was first and foremost interested in creating gay community, which its structure and programs reflected, while the gay medical students were concerned with science, health, and medicine. Despite the culture difference between these two groups, the benefits of collaboration drew them to one another. Reacting to numerous requests and the gay medical students group's growing reputation as gay medical advocates, Gay Horizons organizers asked if the gay medical students group would offer free testing and education during an organization-sponsored weekly coffeehouse event where gays and lesbians could gather, read poetry, and mingle in a space rented by Gay Horizons. With Wissner willing to assume liability, the free coffee shop space, and a group of medical students ready to volunteer their time and services, the student group began offering weekly VD testing. Even as the two groups had different, though complementary missions, a mutually beneficial collaboration grew out of Gay Horizons' desire to expand into a full social service organization and the gay medical students group's plan to provide VD testing.

Like the early days in Boston's Fenway Community Health Clinic and the Los Angeles Gay Community Services Center, the coffeehouse "clinic" reflected the needs of the gay male community, the relaxed regulation of community health services, and the entrepreneurialism of gay health activists of the period. One of the medical students group's most active early members (besides Ostrow) was Kenneth Mayer, a medical student at Northwestern University. In just his second year of school, Mayer jumped at the chance to work with patients and volunteered weekly to do exams and conduct testing. He commented in an interview, "In retrospect this was something we would never allow now . . . because my training was minimal, I was really early in my medical training and the level of supervision was really minimal but you kind of quick-study. It was a really incredible learning experience."[70] In 1980, after finishing medical school, Mayer moved to Boston, where he became instrumental in transforming the Fenway clinic into a world-class research institution. The casual, make-do approach to staffing permeated nearly every aspect of the clinic, which consisted of "a coffee pot, a portable kitchen table, [and] a room above an old grocery market."[71] Ostrow explained how the ethos translated into the health services:

> Wednesday evening once a week . . . We were mostly medical students and a couple of residents and maybe a couple of actually licensed MDs. So we couldn't really officially be a treatment site, but we would try to have a doctor there every Wednesday night, and if there was a doctor there he would write a prescription for medication. But if we couldn't get a doctor there or the patient didn't have money for the prescription, we would actually pilfer the medications from the stockrooms at our hospitals where we were training.[72]

Mayer concurred, "There was a lot of begging, borrowing, and stealing," just as had been the case in Boston.[73]

Within months of its opening the gay health clinic also began to go by its own name, which reflected the mutual medical and gay liberation roots of group members: the Howard Brown Memorial Clinic. Howard Brown had been the head of the New York City Health Services Administration in the mid-1960s, charged with managing dozens of hospitals and clinics and thousands of employees before he chose to step down rather than be outed by an investigative reporter in 1967. From there he went on to join the faculty at area medical schools before he announced his homosexuality at a lecture at one such school in 1973. His coming out made the front page of the *New York Times*, and he became the highest profile gay medical professional in an era in which simply being homosexual was cause for medical concern.[74] Brown embodied the changing attitude toward homosexuality within medicine that gay health activists around the country worked toward throughout the 1970s.[75] In early 1975, shortly after the gay medical students' clinic began operation, Brown died at the age of fifty of a heart attack. The students named their coffee shop clinic in homage to the greatest gay doctor activist of their time.

The Howard Brown Memorial Clinic grew, moving from its initial space in the Gay Horizons coffee shop above the grocery store in the fall of 1975 to an office in the La Plaza Medical Center that could accommodate increased hours of operation that spilled over into two nights per week.[76] Even with its successful diagnosis and treatment of hundreds of cases of venereal diseases, the work of the clinic was reactive in nature. Though gay men came to the clinic because they were, or thought they were, infected with a venereal disease, the majority of the gay community did not frequent the clinic. With his knowledge of social medicine, gained from mentors at the University of Chicago (which included social medicine authority Dr. Quentin Young), Ostrow knew that "if you want to rob, you go to banks because that's where the money is. So if you want to get people and test them and treat them before they pass on VD, you go to places where they're congregating . . . and having sex . . . you have to go to where the people are rather than wait for them to come to you."[77] In other words, to make health care within the gay community more preventative, rather than reactive, and instill a concern for sexual health among the growing gay social and sexual culture, the Howard Brown Memorial Clinic needed to provide services and build relationships beyond the walls of the new clinic space. Here again, as the clinic sought to start outreach programs with gay bars and businesses to attract new patients and conduct research, the threads of gay liberation and medicine intertwined in Chicago.

Though clearly medical in its focus, the Howard Brown Memorial Clinic relied heavily on the city's blossoming gay businesses and institutions to bring its services to fruition at first and to expand them. Its initial affiliation with Gay Horizons, along with the personal reputations of clinic activists, gained the clinic access and permission to conduct outreach in local bars and bathhouses. Even as a subsidiary of the larger organization, the clinic was largely autonomous. The medical students scheduled their own volunteers to staff the clinic, managed patient "files," which consisted of hundreds of four-by-six-inch index cards, and ferried blood samples to city labs.[78] As their self-sufficiency grew, with the clinic leaving the coffeehouse venue for a larger, more conducive space that could accommodate increased hours of operation, the priorities of Gay Horizons and the Howard Brown Memorial Clinic diverged from one another. The clinic focused on medical services and research, and it grew exponentially in its first two years in patient numbers, outreach possibilities, and potential for scientific study.[79] True to his training as both a medical doctor and a biochemist, Ostrow began conducting medical research, proposing large-scale studies, and, later, publishing his findings to advance knowledge about gay sexual practices, medical needs, and effective treatment methods shortly after the clinic opened.[80] Meanwhile, Gay Horizons' interests lay in building community and providing social services to Chicago gays and lesbians. It began in 1973 by creating a gay helpline and providing meeting spaces like the coffee house that also housed the clinic. Over the course of the next three years, the organization shifted its focus from building social community to also providing social support services like a youth program, peer counseling service, and a drop-in center.[81] The inclusion of VD testing in the coffeehouse in 1974 speaks to the organization's move to provide more support services to the gay community during this period. By 1976, Gay Horizons, in its service offerings, was reminiscent of, though smaller and without a large building of its own, the Los Angeles Gay Community Services Center. By contrast, the Howard Brown Memorial Clinic edged closer to being a medical clinic and research facility. The divergent missions proved grating.

A funding dispute in 1976 allowed the clinic to break away from Gay Horizons and create a clear set of policies and procedures that reflected its allegiance to efficient, high-quality medical care as well as to the gay community. The Howard Brown Memorial Clinic employed a very structured and traditional organizational model with a set board of directors, to which people were nominated, including officer positions of treasurer, secretary, and medical director, among others. The rigid and hierarchical organizational structure chosen by the clinic contrasts dramatically with the Fenway clinic's original structure in Boston. In fact, also unlike in Los Angeles, there appears to have been very little debate of any other structure or alternative hierarchy for the Chicago clinic, illustrating the strong medical, rather than political, roots of the clinic and its volunteers.

In the place of concern and debate over organizational structures and everyday operations, the medical students and professionals of the Howard Brown Memorial Clinic, with Ostrow at the lead, almost immediately set their sights on medical research and quickly took up the mantle as the most research-focused gay community health clinic in the country. Ostrow and other medical students and young medical professionals like Ken Mayer created an ethos for the new organization that relied on medical training and scientific research to address the medical needs of the gay community. Ostrow and others also made sure that the clinic continued to provide free and sliding-scale services as a gesture to their shared political belief in socialized medicine. This strong set of guiding principles that focused on providing low-cost, quality medical care while furthering medical and scientific knowledge, remained the driving force for the clinic as it grew throughout the 1970s. While not completely in the shadows, gay liberation clearly acted in a more complementary or supporting role to the dedication to medicine that spurred gay health activism in Chicago. The social- and services-focused gay liberation politics of Chicago allowed the clinic to draw on gay liberation activism when it made sense to propel the medical mission of the clinic forward.

Boston's Fenway Community Health Clinic, Los Angeles's Gay Community Services Center, and Chicago's Howard Brown Memorial Clinic each reflected its local politics and community much more than any national gay liberation movement. Even as each of these clinics became a gay institution that continues to thrive today, with strong ties to the gay community and national gay political efforts, they all began as precarious ideas designed to address particular local problems that were often only incidentally or tangentially related to gay liberation. From this perspective, "gay liberation" appears as a complex collage of gay people navigating a variety of local politics rather than as gay people across the country subscribing to and implementing a movement's ideologies and tactics. The 1970s witnessed important shifts of gay physical and political landscapes across the country, but to understand these changes as coordinated or anything more than loosely connected with one another would be to misunderstand them and gay liberation more generally. While gay liberation played an important role in these clinics at times and in different, locally distinctive ways, proclaiming them an example of gay liberation oversimplifies their origins and misrepresents gay liberation. These clinics, though often cast as proud institutions of the gay liberation era, reflect a complicated time, complex people, and multifaceted local political contexts. From this perspective, the gay liberation movement is at once a cacophony of local politics, an ethos, a way of being that has gained much greater imagined clarity, uniformity, and power in the public's hindsight than it ever demonstrated in any of these clinics.

This more dynamic, locally grounded understanding of gay liberation also allows for a decentering of gay liberation in the historical origins of gay services and institutions. While tracing the points of intersection between gay liberation and gay health activism in the 1970s is useful to understanding the local inner workings of gay liberation politics and rhetoric and health activism, looking beyond gay liberation paints a much fuller picture of the politics undergirding gay health activism. Shifting the focus away from gay liberation illuminates the many ties between gay institutions (like gay health clinics) and a wide variety of social and political movements of the period. In the light of those connections, the history of gay health activism transforms from a "gay history," or even a history of sexuality, to a history of the 1970s and 1980s.

CHAPTER 2

BEYOND GAY LIBERATION

The language and ideas of gay health activism were less often local expressions of gay liberation than articulations shared with various social and political movements. Indeed, the activism and politics around gay health appeared to be the products of a great political cross-pollination among groups, movements, and ideologies of the period. National debates and policies related to stemming poverty and increasing access to health care expanded into gay health clinics, far beyond the desks of politicians, bureaucrats, and urban developers. Critiques of capitalism and the state it mechanized laced the politics of those who would become gay health activists. Sexual liberation and feminism, two hallmarks of this period, laid important cultural and material groundwork as they shifted societal sexual norms and created countless new community spaces, without which gay health activism could not have blossomed. While institutions that bolstered gay liberation ideals and existed alongside many other institutions inspired by gay liberation were often the end result of this activism, the historical origins of gay health activism actually decenter gay liberation, revealing a complex and politically blended landscape that essentially reflects the history of 1970s social movements.

Money Matters

Critiques of capitalism proved a driving force in gay health activism and seeped into it through numerous movements across the social justice spectrum that linked capitalism to injustice and suffering. In Boston, gentrification and urban renewal had clear ties to capitalism, posing a threat to the Fenway neighborhood and fueling the activism that ultimately provided gay health services in the city. Fenway's dilapidated housing stood in stark contrast to some of the city's most important cultural landmarks. The Fens, a large park created in the late 1800s by renowned landscape architect Frederick Law Olmsted, lay at the heart of the area, serving as a bucolic destination on its own but also attracting other cultural landmarks to the neighborhood, including the Fenway Park baseball stadium, the Boston Museum of Fine Arts, the New England Conservatory of Music, and numerous college campuses.[1] The desire to capitalize on the "outstanding potential" of the neighborhood, in the words of the Boston Redevelopment Authority, translated into pressure from landlords, developers, and city officials for Fenway residents to vacate and make way for "higher-income, higher-quality housing."[2] Capitalist forces drove many in real estate, development, and local government in the 1960s and 1970s to make living in the Fenway, and in countless similar urban neighborhoods across the country, uncomfortable, unsafe, and untenable. Fenway residents experienced dozens of fires, killing five people and making hundreds more homeless, as landlords and even fire marshals attempted to cash in crumbling apartment buildings for lucrative insurance payouts and kickbacks from developers.[3] Between 1969 and 1974 the neighborhood saw reports of arson increase by more than 1200 percent.[4] Capitalism, with its emphasis on profits and exploitation of the poor, emerged as an obvious and galvanizing enemy as area activists banded together to repel the developers and improve their neighborhood in ways that benefited existing residents, including founding the Fenway Community Health Clinic. One Fenway resident offered a telling analogy: "In the south it was sheriffs and dogs. But you look at who was the oppressor up in this part of the world, and it was the developer."[5]

The antiwar movement, fortified by critiques of capitalism and questions about the true motivations of the Cold War, also provided the bedrock upon which gay health activists built their clinics and networks. The movement honed the skills of many of the most vocal activists in Boston, Chicago, Los Angeles, and elsewhere, instilling in them strong critiques of the state and war profiteering. Chicago's David Ostrow described the antiwar movement on the University of Chicago campus and in the larger city as "pretty radicalizing"; it was through that movement that he became conscious of medicine's potential as a tool for social justice.[6] At the encouragement of his colleagues in a university laboratory where he worked as an undergraduate researcher in the summer of 1968, Ostrow joined members of the Medical Committee for Human Rights in providing first aid to protesters amid the riots that broke out in Chicago's Grant Park during the Democratic National Convention over the party's position on the Vietnam War. Those summer days and nights of administering bandages illuminated clearly for Ostrow the relationship between antiwar activism, capitalism, and medicine and gave him a political orientation that shaped his life's work, and the work of the Howard Brown Memorial Clinic that he helped found just six years later. He found ways to channel his passion for medicine to also address political inequalities. Antiwar activism also served as the impetus for friendships and coalitions that would prove crucial to the emergence of gay health clinics in the years that followed, such as the relationship between David Scondras and Linda Beane in Boston, and the coalitions and reputation built by Morris Kight through his work as the founder of the DOW Action Committee, a group dedicated to stopping the production and use of napalm in the Vietnam War.[7] The critical thinking and organizing skills activists gained through the antiwar movement filtered into the gay health clinics that emerged during the 1970s around the country.

The political battles over socialized medicine, again based on critiques of capitalism, molded the political landscape in which gay health activism grew. While the 1965 Medicaid and Medicare legislation made health care accessible to millions who previously found the cost and proximity to care a hindrance (Medicaid offered a partial medical safety net for very poor single women and children, while Medicare offered a fuller one to the elderly), it reinvigorated the socialized medicine movement when it failed to make health care free and accessible to all. By the early 1970s, the National Free Clinic Council's ranks swelled with free clinics, among them many catering to gay patients, that both highlighted and ameliorated the flaws of the legislation. Little oversight and limitless reimbursements led many Medicare providers to charge the government exorbitant prices for tests, treatments, and procedures that were often excessive, redundant, or unnecessary for their elderly patients. Thus, federal and state governments watched their health-care budgets explode with unnecessary and fraudulent Medicare claims as patients often received care driven more by profits than by medicine.[8] One newspaper article summarized the problem in 1974 thus: "Some physicians were raking in hundreds of thousands of tax dollars a year and no mechanism existed to measure the quality of care they were giving—or indeed even to determine that they were giving care at all."[9] Meanwhile, Medicaid offered paltry reimbursements for physicians and hospitals, translating into a shrinking number of Medicaid providers for poor women and children and a reluctance to order expensive diagnostics or treatments. As a result, many Medicare and Medicaid patients were not receiving quality medical care either because their doctors were more interested in making a profit than providing proper care or because cash-strapped states began to limit enrollment in the Medicaid program in a poor attempt to decrease their health-care costs.[10]

Gay men felt the realities of the shifting health-care landscape in multiple ways. Medicaid, though designed as a social safety measure for the poor, had very specific and heteronormative qualifications that almost exclusively covered extremely poor single women and children.[11] Men, at least those without severe disabilities, did not qualify for the program and thus fell through the Medicaid social safety net. However, gay men often did not experience employment (or the access to health care) in the same way that the law assumed men would, since workplace homophobia and discrimination meant that gay men often had more difficulty finding and keeping jobs. When employed, gay men often turned to underfunded public health clinics to avoid friends, families, and employers learning of their sexual practices, which often resulted in job loss. Thus, gay men either lacked private health insurance or could be outed by using it. As states reduced funding for these public health clinics, gay men's access to health care became even more precarious. They were caught between homophobic employment-based health insurance that didn't allow them to be out and poorly funded state clinics intended to serve poor women and children. This structural inequity resulted not from explicit antigay legislation, but rather from the assumption that all men were heterosexual. Thus, while gay men faced the additional barrier of homophobia within mainstream medicine, mainstream medicine's ties to capitalism and the state also blocked their access to quality care.

The national political focus on poverty during the 1960s and 1970s fueled activism for socialized medicine within communities that experienced poverty, like the Fenway, and within the medical profession itself.[12] On one side, the American Medical Association (AMA) favored the existing medical system, claiming that it furthered medical innovation and research while also giving individual doctors the greatest possible freedom in their medical practice. [13] On the other side, proponents for socialized medicine, including a large Chicago contingent that oriented David Ostrow's political compass, argued that health care should be easily accessible to all, rather than contingent upon insurance or income, and that medicine was an important tool in fighting social inequality and injustice. Their interest in providing health care to all led socialized medicine proponents to integrate more public health tactics into their medical practice, including creating community health clinics, conducting outreach, and focusing on prevention. Socialized medicine politics motivated the health practitioners who pioneered gay health services across the country, from Milwaukee's Gay Clinic to the public health outreach collaborations between Chicago's Howard Brown Memorial Clinic and area bars and bathhouses. The national debate over access to affordable, quality health care made the gay health services of the 1970s possible.

Over the course of the 1970s and 1980s, despite the anticapitalist dreams of many of the activists, gay health services and clinics could not avoid the effects of capitalism. In Los Angeles, the realities of capitalism and the importance of state support in ensuring the Gay Community Services Center's longevity tempered that clinic's founding ideals from the start. In Boston, the Fenway Community Health Clinic clung to its anticapitalist roots for as long as possible. Beyond a federal seed grant, most of which had been spent on transforming the abandoned antique shop into a suitable clinic space, and a federal fund-matching program with Deaconess Hospital that provided the Fenway clinic with a small medical staff and grants for medical supplies, the clinic had no other immediate sources of income. [14] Scondras remarked, "We would steal equipment and medicines for the health center because we didn't have a way to buy them, and that couldn't go on forever." [15] In 1973, just a few months after opening the clinic, some volunteers broached the topic of charging for services in one of the town hall–style board meetings. While charging for services seemed a likely and obvious source of badly needed revenue for the struggling clinic, the idea was in direct opposition to the founding ideals of the clinic, and the resulting debate was both long and contentious. Providing free health care had been as much an organizing principle for the clinic as preserving the Fenway neighborhood had been. [16] Factions quickly developed between those who felt it a necessity to sustain the clinic and those who felt it "would violate a principle that health care should be free for everyone." [17] One volunteer remembered, "In our minds, the 50 cent fee would lead to corruption and bureaucracy!"[18] However, after more than twenty-four hours of debate spread over several board meetings, idealism bent under the weight of the harsh fiscal reality the clinic faced.[19] The Fenway volunteers and community members settled on a compromise agreement whereby the clinic would charge fifty cents per visit with the caveat that patients who either couldn't or didn't want to pay the fee could either volunteer in return for services or pay whatever they could afford.[20] The deal preserved the clinic's identity as a free clinic while also placing it on slightly better financial ground.

Just as the Fenway clinic community crafted an acceptable compromise for one ideological challenge rooted in capitalism and anticapitalism politics, another surfaced. Toward the end of 1973, a fight over whether to hire its first paid staff dominated the board meetings. The battle with the Boston Redevelopment Authority had hinged on the political belief that all Fenway residents should have the same rights and political value to the state as the wealthy residents the redevelopment plan hoped to attract. This sentiment filtered into the ethos of the clinic. Volunteers were uncomfortable paying some for work that others did for free, since it could easily be interpreted as the Fenway community placing greater value on one volunteer over the other, or valuing one form of qualifications or training above another. Paying staff seemed to many a slippery slope where judgments over who to hire and for how much pay could easily clash with the ideals of the clinic.[21] Again, after many hours of debate the board settled on a compromise whereby staff could be paid, but "everyone made the same hourly wage, no matter what you did."[22] The first paid Fenway staff was physician's assistant Ron Vachon, who also helped coordinate volunteers.[23] Within a year, the clinic had ten paid staff: some doctors, some physician's assistants, and other former volunteers who assisted with clerical work. Longtime volunteer physician Lenny Alberts recalled, "It was a big deal when we started getting $10 a session, though, of course, we were encouraged to donate it all back into the pot."[24] Board members endorsed this unconventional pay scale as an attempt to preserve the ideal that every person regardless of education, job, or experience had the same worth and value to the greater community. Yet market pressures again demanded change just a few years later in 1980 as a doctor shortage forced the Fenway clinic to pay its medical staff on a graduated scale in the interest of retaining doctors and nurses.[25] Living out anticapitalist ideals proved increasingly difficult as the decade progressed, but anticapitalism politics and its related movements in the 1970s left a clear and influential mark on 1970s gay health activism and would reemerge in the early AIDS crisis of the 1980s.

Intersecting Identities

Identity-based political movements proved equally influential in molding gay health activism in the 1970s. While most histories of gay activism during this period place gay liberation at the center, a close exploration of gay health activism and its related institutions shows that the ideas and tactics born of many other identity-based movements also molded it, sometimes to a much greater degree than gay liberation. The Black Panthers, Brown Berets, the American Indian Movement, and feminism, as well as gay liberation, each proved an important factor in the development of gay health services in the decade.

The transmission of ideas among these movements varied widely. In Boston, Beane and Scondras's inspiring visit to the Black Panther Health Clinic that led to their opening the Fenway neighborhood clinic exemplifies direct interactions between groups, while identity-based movements shaped the Los Angeles Gay Community Services Center by very different means. Don Kilhefner proved an individual catalyst between the politics of the Black Panthers and the emerging center. When Kilhefner arrived in Los Angeles in 1969 it was the last in a series of moves that had spanned much of the decade and taken him around the world. As one of the first volunteers for President Kennedy's newly minted Peace Corps program, Kilhefner served in northern Ethiopia from 1962 to 1965 teaching history in a school and helping build other social services for the local community. There, he befriended a number of political activists in the African National Congress who would push his politics further to the left.[26] His work in Ethiopia sparked a deep, lifelong interest in African history that, upon the end of his Peace Corps tour, led him to enroll in the graduate program of the history department at the historically black Howard University in Washington, D.C. There, as one of the few white students, and with his personal connections to the black freedom struggles taking place in Africa, Kilhefner gained a perspective on the turbulent civil rights movement, up-and-coming black nationalism, and the escalating antiwar movement that few of his contemporaries within the mostly white New

Left had. It ultimately had a radicalizing effect on him. He witnessed and participated in many protests of the Vietnam War and engaged in debates and activism around racial inequality that loomed large on campus, in the city, and internationally. Explaining the importance of this period in his political formation, Kilhefner recalled, "My consciousness was changing so that I was becoming more aware about power politics . . . in a way that I never had been before."[27] As Kilhefner moved to Los Angeles to pursue his doctorate at the University of California, Los Angeles, he quickly became involved in gay activism there and brought a political perspective shaped by the antiwar and civil rights movements as well as Black Power.

Kilhefner's personal history and political perspective resonated with that of West Coast radicals from numerous movements who framed their political struggle as a life-or-death battle. Black nationalists, feminists, American Indians, and Chicano/a activists all organized around the belief that the white, heterosexual male dominated society and the state were literally killing off their communities. In the wake of the 1965 Watts uprising in south-central Los Angeles, black activists sought to address the many issues that threatened black survival, ranging from the overt threats posed by police violence to the more insidious forms of institutional oppression like the absence of health care, nutritious foods, and basic social services.[28] Feminists in this period couched their battles over reproductive rights in the context of survival, with white women pointing to the health risks of illegal abortion practices and women of color equating forced and uninformed sterilizations with racial genocide.[29] The American Indian Movement mobilized around the state's centuries-old attack on their peoples. Facing the continued colonization of their tribal nations and cultures, activists demanded recognition of tribal sovereignty, called for reforms of the Indian Health Service, and reclaimed lands, most famously with the occupation of Alcatraz Island in San Francisco in 1969.[30] Chicano activists organized around the issues of immigrant rights, safety, workers' rights, and access to social services in movements ranging from the United Farm Workers to the Brown Berets.[31] These activists fought not only for more political rights and power. They also fought for personal protection, community spaces, and social services necessary to avoid their extinction. Community survival made health, education, and safety barometers of oppression. Consequently, health became a powerful organizing tool and a central part of the political identities of each of these movements.

In short, these movements defined health broadly and then equated it with their political liberation. From the perspective of politicized health, homophobia, patriarchy, racism and white ethnocentrism were all symptoms of the same sickness that infected people through oppression. The oppression sickness concept developed by the Gay Survival Committee in the earliest meetings of what would grow to be the Los Angeles Gay Community Services Center similarly pushed beyond the rigid boundaries of a medical understanding of health and illness, blurring the lines between medical and political issues. While the term oppression sickness was unique to gay activists in Los Angeles, it clearly derived from the framing of health as political liberation common among other radical movements active in Los Angeles during this period.

Despite the important influence of identity-movement groups in shaping their activism, gay health activists often failed to design their services in ways that also fought structural racism. Rather, the vast majority of gay health services and clinics that emerged during this period employed a sort of color-blind approach to addressing racial health discrepancies within the gay community. With good intentions, most white activists, who also made up the majority of the leading activists in gay health activism at this time, proclaimed "everyone" welcome and went about tailoring and promoting services to meet the needs of the gay community based on their own experiences.[32] However, they failed to recognize, as was common in majority white services and movements of the period, that people of color or low-income people might have different needs or respond to alternate forms of outreach designed specifically with them in mind. Though no clinic appeared overtly racist and each had a smattering of patients of color that allowed it to claim a racially diverse clientele, those who used gay health services across the country proved overwhelmingly white.[33] This even held true for the gay health services at the Fenway clinic, despite the fact that all the clinic's other services drew a very racially and economically diverse clientele throughout the 1970s.[34]

Sexism proved equally prevalent and often more overt despite the significance of feminist organizations and activism in the history of gay health activism. Across the country, feminist women's health activism blazed a trail in the late 1960s and early 1970s on which gay health activism frequently followed, often in loose partnership with the lesbians that worked in both movements. Like the efforts of other political movements of the day, women's health activism highlighted the ways in which mainstream medicine served as a tool of oppression, specifically patriarchy.[35] Within the feminist spaces created by the larger women's movement and the political discourse encouraged by radical feminism, women became increasingly critical of the ways in which mainstream medicine reinforced a patriarchal, racist, and often misogynistic society. In addition to the call for specific services, women shed light on the systemic ways in which mainstream medicine reinforced patriarchy by criticizing the limited number of female medical school graduates, medical school curriculum, and medical research that maintained or contributed to women's oppression.[36] As a whole, the women's health movement tackled a broad spectrum of issues, including coerced sterilization, access to quality medical care, abortion rights, rape, family planning, and self-help.[37] Yet, the movement and its participants were often divided along lines of race, class, or reproductive issue, which also allowed them to be more easily excluded or minimized by emerging gay health clinics and service providers.

Boston emerged as an important national hub for feminist health activism, to such an extent that, throughout the 1970s, the Fenway clinic saw its women's health services suffer from lackluster attendance and flagging enthusiasm. Fenway's inclusion of women's health initiatives seemed necessary as part of its attempt to serve the entire neighborhood in the face of renewal efforts, but against the backdrop of the city's robust feminist health offerings, including the Women's Health Book Collective, the Cambridge Women's Center, and the Women's Education Center, such initiatives proved redundant and underutilized. From this perspective, women's health, while included and prioritized, was on unequal footing with most of the clinic's other offerings, especially the gay men's health services, which were the only such services in the entire region. Similarly, Chicago's Howard Brown Memorial Clinic drew on local feminist critiques of mainstream medicine to bolster and validate its existence. In fact, the earliest gay health organizing in Chicago, the advertisement encouraging interested people to call an anonymous phone number, evokes the protocols used by Chicago's Jane Collective to provide abortions before they became legal. However, the clinic itself proved exclusionary of women by unapologetically offering services solely for gay men, arguing that their health needs were far different, less complicated, and required fewer resources than those of women. After numerous requests and a number of letters to the editor in local gay newspapers, the clinic began offering gynecological services in 1978 but did little to welcome or reach out to women, and the program struggled.[38] These clinics showcased a sort of insidious structural sexism that placed women at the peripheries.

In a botched attempt to bridge the historic divide between Los Angeles' gay and lesbian communities, the Gay Community Services Center co-opted feminism and feminist services in new ways that proved detrimental not only to women but also to the institution. Like Boston, Los Angeles served as a hotbed for feminist health activism and the birthplace for many feminist self-help health initiatives that welcomed women and encouraged their participation in their own health care.[39] The clinic's concept of oppression sickness and the do-it-yourself approach to quality services echoed the politics and efforts of multiple feminist and women's health initiatives across the city. However, from the very start of the Los Angeles Gay Community Services Center in 1971, lesbians found themselves at the margins. While the Los Angeles Center was its own entity, it was an outgrowth of the local Gay Liberation Front (GLF) chapter, and the center's founders and many of its board members were GLF veterans. GLF had, in its short two-year existence, earned a reputation among lesbian activists as an organization dominated by men who were often sexist and inconsiderate of women's issues. Alienated female former GLF members had started many of the city's women's services, like those at the Gay Women's Service Center, where lesbians could find a safe place to sleep in the face of violence or homelessness, rap groups, potlucks, and self-defense classes.[40] As the founders of the Los Angeles Gay Community Services Center set their sights on becoming the city's gay and lesbian headquarters in the interest of consolidating area political power and resources, they hoped to subsume existing lesbian services and organizations. With their exclusion from GLF meetings and decisions fresh in their memories, many Los Angeles lesbian activists, including Sharon Raphael and Mina Meyer, the driving forces behind the Gay Women's Service Center, proved reluctant to give up their own newly created spaces and organizations to become incorporated in the Gay Community Services Center.

Rooted firmly in the belief that gay men and lesbians "share a common oppression and that our capacity to be free and proud is also dependent on how much we stick together . . . as sisters or brothers, to become part of our growing community," Gay Community Services Center founders Morris Kight and Don Kilhefner were not deterred by lesbian disinterest in their vision.[41] Rather, they employed many tactics, most of which only exacerbated tensions and skepticism between Los Angeles gays and lesbians, to make the center's old Victorian building in the Silver Lake neighborhood the heart of gay and lesbian politics and services in the city. Kight repeatedly went to the Gay Women's Service Center to convince Meyer and Raphael to join the Gay Community Services Center. However, the women had concerns "join[ing] with the men because we felt something would be lost." [42] When they rebuffed his offer, the Gay Community Services Center took more aggressive action to force the lesbians to join the center. Management scheduled the center's women's rap groups to occur on the same night of the week as those held at the Gay Women's Service Center, in effect pitting the two organizations against one another. Immediately, the Gay Women's Service Center saw a drop in attendance as many women opted to go to the Gay Community Services Center. Unlike the collectively run Gay Women's Service Center, the Gay Community Services Center, with its numerous volunteers, did not require visitors to do any chores or work for the organization. Raphael explained, "The women liked it over there because they didn't have to do any work."[43] As a result of dwindling numbers and steady pressure from Kight and Kilhefner, the women of the Gay Women's Service Center realized that merging with the Gay Community Services Center "was inevitable."[44] Raphael and Meyer watched for six months before finally deciding to close the Gay Women's Service Center. Raphael recalled the sentiment behind the decision: "Eventually they just wore us down . . . we were basically following the women who had left us."[45]

While the actions of the Gay Community Services Center were obviously hostile and designed to force the closure of the Gay Women's Service Center, the leaders of both groups sought to make the eventual merger a smooth one in the spirit of creating a stronger gay and lesbian community. Raphael explained how the women "knew we were being co-opted, we knew what was going on."[46] Meyer added, "We figured we'd try it and see how it felt."[47] In a good faith gesture, Raphael and Meyer donated all the furniture from the Gay Women's Service Center to the new organization when the former finally closed its doors. Meanwhile, Kight and Kilhefner offered both Meyer and Raphael positions in management upon their arrival at the Gay Community Services Center in an effort to assuage their concerns about sexism within their new home. Mina Meyer became vice president of the board of directors and the head of all women's programs, while Sharon Raphael took a position as head of research. Raphael shed light on the Janus-faced aspect of the sexually integrated center: "Even though there was this male-female dynamic, we were very close to the men. . . . It was a very community atmosphere."[48]

As the vice president of the board of directors, Meyer did her best to make sure that roughly half of the programs offered by the center in the early part of the decade were either specifically for or open to lesbians. The center offered the weekly women's dances, potlucks, and rap groups previously offered by the Gay Women's Service Center.[49] However, many of the services that were open to lesbians *and* gay men drew an almost entirely male population. Furthermore, some of the center's largest and most popular programs, like a program that provided assistance for former military personnel who had been dishonorably discharged for being gay, services for prisoners, and VD testing, were for an almost exclusively male population. Even some of the center's largest programs served a predominantly gay clientele, although they were officially open to lesbians. The Van Ness House, which offered housing and treatment services for gay and lesbian alcoholics, consisted almost entirely of men.[50]

The center's funding procedures and laissez-faire approach to program development did little to embody feminist ideals or assuage lesbian exclusion. Within this structure, the board and management oversaw building management, staffing, and the general budget. However, volunteers created individual programs, sought board approval, and then generally designed, implemented, staffed, advertised, and found necessary funding for each individual program.[51] The center simply provided space and volunteers. As Meyer struggled to create many new programs at once in order to provide greater gender equity in the center's offerings, she and other lesbians interpreted this hands-off approach on the part of the center as further proof of its lack of concern for women's issues and services. Her frustration became palpable nearly forty years later as she recounted in an interview her efforts to create a gynecological clinic: "If you are going to have a men's clinic you should have a women's clinic. . . . And they said, 'Well, if you want to find your own doctors and your own nurses and your own technicians and if you want to put it together go ahead, you know, we're not going to help you do it but if you want to do it, we'll get you the space for it.'"[52] The center's hands-off, fend-for-yourself response to Meyer's idea for a women's clinic, though typical, struck her and other lesbians as "totally sexist and unhelpful."[53] In fact, in 1973 Meyer "left the center because of the sexism that was going on. It was just intolerable."[54] On her departure she left a number of new programs for women, including a women's health clinic that would flounder and close months later because of lack of support from the center, and mounting tensions between the center's lesbians and gays.[55] This and many more divisions between the sexes at the center in coming years demonstrate another way in which gay health service organizations drew from feminist framings, politics, and services in their origins yet often reinforced sexism in their practices.[56]

Gay Liberation

Though various other political movements proved pivotal in the development of gay health services in the 1970s, gay liberation also provided an integral piece in the political puzzle. In Boston, burgeoning gay businesses and social outlets both precipitated the need for gay health services and effectively spread word of them throughout the city and region. Internally, gay liberation played a nominal role in the creation and growth of the Fenway clinic itself as most of its gay activists remained at least partially closeted and only tangentially affiliated with gay liberation activism. In Los Angeles, gay liberation, more specifically the creation of gay spaces and services, proved a strong internal motivation for the Gay Community Services Center and its predecessor, the Gay Helpline. The Los Angeles Gay Community Services Center applied the political framing from numerous other local and national movements to the creation of gay services and community, their ultimate goal.

Chicago's Howard Brown Memorial Clinic had a more complex relationship to gay liberation. Research and outreach appeared both integral and interrelated in Chicago from the clinic's start, unlike in other locations. This interest in outreach contributed to the bars and bathhouses of Chicago becoming visible, if somewhat improbable, venues for gay sexual health in the 1970s. In fact, many of the city's gay bars and bathhouses shared the clinic's interest in providing outreach services. Their interest in the sexual health of their patrons was twofold. Health services were a business interest for bars and, particularly, bathhouses. Gary Chichester, longtime manager of the largest bathhouse in the Midwest, Man's Country, explained how venereal diseases were bad for businesses built on gay sex and sexuality: "If people are naked and had a [syphilis sore], they are not going to be parading around."[57] Providing these services meant that "people were actually on top of it and they actually appreciated the fact that we were doing something to help because the sex was good but we were protecting them also, opening up their minds, and giving them information."[58] However, business and profits were not the only forces at work behind the creation of gay health outreach programs in Chicago. Rather, the collaboration between bars and bathhouses from the inception of these programs suggests that the historical role of bars and bathhouses as community centers for the larger gay community also were a motivating factor.[59] Man's Country owner and gay businessman Chuck Renslow explained, "This is family, my community, we're together . . . you can't just worry about your bar, you've got to worry about the total picture."[60] In the summer of 1975, as the Howard Brown Memorial Clinic was preparing to move and expand its hours, Chichester and Renslow created what would become the most important outreach program for Chicago gay health in the 1970s— the VD van program.

The concept was simple: every couple of months, local gay businesses, mainly bars and bathhouses, would financially contribute to renting a Winnebago van that would travel to each business and provide free VD testing. Chichester later recalled in an interview, "My thinking was: it is something that is curable, it is something that is out there, let's talk about it, and let's take care of it."[61] Setting the groundwork for the program, Renslow and Chichester first approached a number of managers and owners of large bars and bathhouses in the Chicago area to gain the necessary support of the business community. Having established an interest in the program, they reached out to the Howard Brown Memorial Clinic, by then already reputable despite having been open only a little more than a year, in search of volunteers capable of conducting the testing. This initiated a relationship between the clinic and the gay bars and bathhouses of the city that would continue for decades, and illuminates the important role gay liberation played in the development of the clinic. Having all the necessary community support and staffing, Renslow rented a large van that volunteers then filled with testing kits, a cooler for blood work and samples, and a handful of knowledgeable medical staff. Participating businesses and local newspapers advertised the program, yet, in July 1975, "when the van first went out . . . we tested four people."[62]

Gay liberation factored heavily in the collaborative response to the lack-

Figure 5. The Chicago VD van parked in front of a gay bar offering testing to bar patrons. "New VD Clinic in Gay Ghetto? VD Bus Patronage Exceeds Goal," *Chicago Gay Crusader*, 1975, 1, 8. Courtesy of the Gerber/Hart Library and Archives, Chicago.

luster turnout. Renslow and Chichester drew on a local gay liberation icon, a drag queen from Man's Country known as Wanda Lust, who agreed to take on another persona—Nurse Lust—and serve as the poster person for the VD van program. For much of the second half of the 1970s, a poster of the sultry Nurse Lust imploring Chicago gay men with her best Uncle Sam impersonation—"I Want You for a Free VD Test!"—was ubiquitous in gay bars and bathhouses.[63] Nurse Lust was also often on the VD van as it made its stops, bringing with her the campy humor that came to epitomize the program, "She'd walk up to people coming out of the bar and say, 'Come on sweetheart, get tested or I won't let you screw me tonight.'"[64] Chichester remembered how businesses further added to the appeal of the program: "We made it kind of fun . . . we offered them cookies and milk, and they would come on and get the blood test and [nurse] Wanda [Lust] would be there being Wanda, it was fabulous!"[65] The VD van became something that many patrons looked forward to as it came to mean not only an act of sexual self-care, but also something fun. The program quickly became so popular that the VD van became a monthly occurrence and stopped at so many bars and bathhouses that it quickly grew from a one-night start-up to a three-night process, and then finally graduated to a weeklong operation. Renslow remembered the program's success and popularity: "Before it ended, there were lines to get in to be tested."[66]

Figure 6. This iconic and ubiquitous poster advertising the VD van in Chicago hung in most gay bars in the city. VD van program, "I Want You for a Free VD Test," 1976, Walter Lear Personal Collection. Gifted to author as part of oral interview. Walter Lear, interview by author, May, 21, 2007.

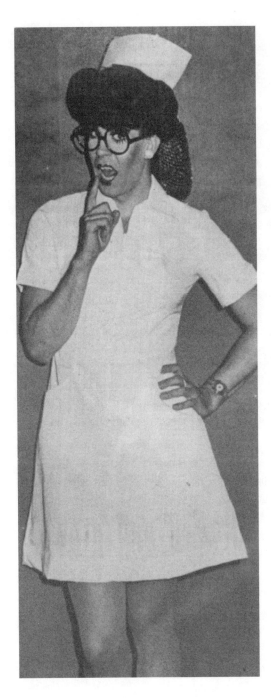

Figure 7. Nurse Wanda Lust. "New VD Clinic in Gay Ghetto? VD Bus Patronage Exceeds Goal," *Chicago Gay Crusader*, 1975, 1, 8. Courtesy of Gerber/Hart Library and Archives, Chicago.

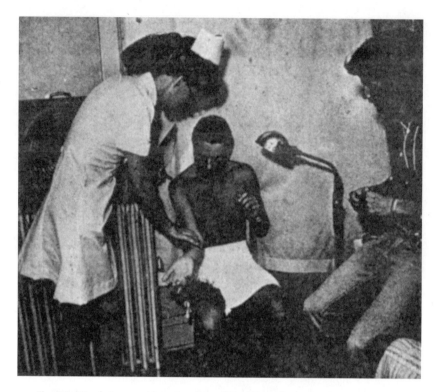

Figure 8. Wanda Lust applying a bandage after a VD test in the Man's Country on-site clinic. "VD Van Is Back," *Gay Life*, May 13, 1977, 1. Courtesy of Gerber/Hart Library and Archives, Chicago.

The VD van program, with its integration of gay liberation businesses, politics, and entertainment, played a significant role in the development of the Howard Brown Memorial Clinic, as it helped build the clinic's reputation among the larger Chicago gay community. By integrating testing with entertainment familiar to the gay community, the program strengthened the relationship between the gay and medical communities in the 1970s. Additionally, it helped solidify the clinic's appeal to city and federal funding sources by allowing the clinic to take much of the credit for staffing the VD van program and other bathhouse outreach programs.[67] As the most effective modes of "prevention" at the time were to educate patrons about disease symptoms and provide access to free testing, the VD van program proved highly effective in containing and treating venereal diseases. Thus, the Howard Brown volunteers teamed with bathhouses and bars to educate the larger gay community and provide services by embracing the politics of sexual freedom and gay liberation.

Gay health activism presents a complex history of the 1970s in which people and institutions previously assumed to be involved in a single identity-based form of activism were in reality drawing on a rich tableau of diverse movements, many of which were grappling with slightly different iterations of the same types of oppression. The direct impact of this cross-pollination of political framing and tactics on the formation and evolution of gay health services challenges the historical narrative that links all gay institutions from this era directly and solely to gay liberation activism. Some gay institutions, like Fenway, did not start out as gay at all, while others, like Howard Brown, became gayer with the help of the local gay community. From this perspective, gay health activism's origins can be traced back to larger discussions of health access, community survival, and the application of activist ideals to seemingly apolitical issues that occurred on a much broader scale in the 1970s. Yet vague political solidarity, borrowed tactics, and shared individual activists rarely translated into race- and feminist-conscious gay health services. Thus, gay health activism illuminates a different kind of gay institution building during the gay liberation period and captures the complexities of exchanging people and ideas across movement borders in a period characterized by increasingly fragmented identity politics.

The political origins of the clinics in Boston, Los Angeles, and Chicago were wildly divergent from one another. Yet, state regulation, licensure requirements, and funding stipulations replaced each clinic's politics with narrow definitions of health and a focus on providing services in a highly medicalized environment, making the clinics fairly similar by the end of the decade. The convergence of these three histories at the end of the period reflects the important role of the state in shaping gay health services and organizations during this period. Indeed by the end of the 1970s, the clinics in Boston, Los Angeles, and Chicago bore much greater resemblance to large social service organizations or medical research institutions than to their meager, more ideologically based origins. The implications of this transformation extend beyond gay health, speaking to the larger role of the state in co-opting or defusing radical social movements, of which the women's health movement may be the best example.[68] Moreover, this history provides for greater debate and discussion of the evolution of social movements during this period, as the clinics' struggles with ideology and sustainability through state funding and involvement mirror the choices activists in many movements faced.

CHAPTER 3

GAY HEALTH HARNESSES THE STATE

The state, defined here as government at local, state, and federal levels, proved just as instrumental to the development of gay health services in the 1970s as the wide array of social movements, including gay liberation, that provided the political catalyst. As a regulator and funder, the state made many gay health clinics possible and then molded them, over the course of the decade, into sustainable entities. Not only did the state facilitate the emergence of gay health services through funding and licensing, but it helped to ensure that gay health services would survive the conservative political swing of the 1980s by forcing clinics' professionalization, regulation, and political pragmatism. Yet the state never intended to support the growth of a gay health network. In fact, the state obstructed homosexuality and nonheteronormative community building in many ways throughout the twentieth century.[1] Moreover, the vast majority of gay health activists saw their work as a critique of and in opposition to the state's historic role in perpetuating structural homophobia. Despite these adversarial stances, the state, both in its actions and in the ways activists enacted its services, played a large, if often unintentional, role in the creation and growth of robust and long-lasting gay health services in the 1970s.

New Applications of Old Services

In the 1970s, many cities used community health clinics to address the health needs of people for whom the existing health-care system failed to provide quality care.[2] The concept of community health clinics gained traction and federal funding during the Johnson administration in the mid-1960s as part of the president's larger Great Society agenda and was one of the few programs to win continued support from the Nixon administration.[3] At the helm of medicine at Cook County Hospital in Chicago, social medicine advocate Quentin Young used his position and political influence to champion free community clinics as an effective way to provide health care to the city's underserved. By 1974, the Chicago Board of Health had over fifty health centers offering free services. However, the vast majority of these clinics had very limited service offerings, most of which were either for prenatal and infant care or for mental health services.[4] As David Ostrow and the other Chicago-area gay medical students began to meet in 1973, the city had fewer than half a dozen community clinics with a wide range of services. These clinics benefited not only from state and municipal funding, but also from federal funding.

As part of this larger system of state-affiliated community health clinics, Chicago had a number of VD testing centers spread out across the city to address the growing epidemic of venereal diseases in the adult population that resulted from the changing sexual mores of the late 1960s. However, as in other cities, these public clinics were no friend to the gay community. The clinics were often "insensitive, overcrowded, and sometimes incompetent," with one person who worked in the city's referral service explaining, "Before we use[d] them . . . we tr[ied] every other resource available."[5] Ostrow echoed the recollections of gay men across the country when he described the reputation of city VD clinics among the gay community as "notorious at that time for not being at all respectful to gay people coming in. I mean over and over again we heard stories about how somebody would ask for an anal or an oral gonorrhea test and the person conducting the test would literally drop their instruments and run out of the room or something."[6]

In fact, in the early 1970s the city health clinics earned such a bad reputation that some gay men tried to determine for themselves if they had a venereal disease before subjecting themselves to the clinics. Before the founding of the gay medical students group, the Mattachine Society, the oldest local gay organization in Chicago, searched for testing alternatives for those unwilling to come out to their doctors and afraid to go to city clinics for VD testing or treatment. The Society hosted a lecture by Chuck Renslow, a prominent community member and owner of numerous gay businesses at the time, on self-testing for venereal diseases. As Renslow made clear, however, without blood work, "there is no sure way [to test accurately]. You can . . . piss in a glass and then piss in another glass. If the first glass is cloudy and the second one is clear you probably have some sort of a urinary infection."[7] Discriminatory and poor-quality care at most public health clinics across the country fueled the need and desire for safe and effective alternatives for gay men.

While state-run public health clinics typically represented more of a threat than a resource for gay men, a few very important exceptions embraced gay health needs in ways that made them central to burgeoning gay enclaves and the creation of a national gay medical infrastructure in the 1970s. Specific public health clinics in San Francisco, Denver, Seattle, and Kansas City went to great lengths, often at the urging of either large surrounding gay communities or partially closeted gay public health officials, to welcome gay clients.[8] These few public clinics that actually provided quality care and welcoming outreach to gay clients became important institutions for local gay communities and valuable contributors to improving gay health education among public health officials across the country. They deployed their profile as gay-friendly state entities to challenge larger systemic homophobia in their local and state governments and also lent legitimacy to nonprofit gay-friendly clinic counterparts across the country through research collaborations and national network building.[9] These important exceptions notwithstanding, the state overwhelmingly fueled the need for gay health services by making gay patients desperate for gay-friendly and knowledgeable health-care alternatives.

The state, though unintentionally, also offered the services that would prove to be the bedrock for the creation of gay health services. Federal and state policies associated with the funding for public clinics, like those in Chicago, Boston, and Los Angeles, required them to provide free testing for all blood samples brought in regardless of the source. Through such programs, the state unintentionally offered a critical service for gay health services in Chicago and in cities across the country at no cost to activists. With pilfered supplies and a federal mandate that city labs had to test their samples for free, the gay medical students in Chicago created a modest but busy clinic that treated over 1,200 patients in its first year in operation. Medical students created the gay-friendly space and the state provided the testing results. In this way, the nascent Howard Brown Memorial Clinic identified and treated cases of both syphilis and gonorrhea at a rate more than three times that of the

Chicago Board of Health clinics, quickly earning legitimacy in the eyes of the city's public health advocates.[10] Almost all nonprofit gay health services of the decade, including those offered at the Fenway Community Health Clinic in Boston and at the Los Angeles Gay Community Services Center, also took advantage of free public health laboratory services to process their blood samples, touting record results as well. The public health laboratories and the state stipulations that they test all samples allowed gay health activists to build their own health services while sidestepping the costs of establishing their own labs or paying for results from contracted facilities.

By the time the Howard Brown Memorial Clinic opened in 1974, the Fenway clinic in Boston and the clinic in the Los Angeles Gay Community Services Center had provided anonymity to their patients upon request for years. However, the Howard Brown Memorial Clinic made it a universal practice, used for all patients.[11] While this brought great comfort to the larger gay community and helped build trust between the clinic and gay men in Chicago, it had the opposite effect on the city's public health officials, who, Ostrow later remembered, "of course . . . objected." The Department of Health was "very heavy-handed in case tracking systems. We had tons of reports of doctors or public health [workers] who would say if you don't give us a list of every single sexual partner and how to contact them for the last so many months, we're not going to treat you."[12] For many gay men, especially those not totally out, the prospect of having to reveal so much sensitive information and potentially have their sexuality exposed proved too great a risk. As a result, many avoided going to the doctor or clinic, which only worsened and complicated the effects of the VD epidemic for the gay community.[13] Anonymous testing offered a solution for gay patients that also rendered the usual epidemiological methods for disease tracing useless and left doctors and public health officials relatively powerless in what had previously been a situation in which they had total control.

The frustrated city officials could do little other than voice their concerns as the regulations regarding federal funding and community health clinics that grew out of the Great Society programs of the 1960s and continued to get approval during the Nixon and Carter administrations insisted that government laboratories test all samples brought in from community clinics.[14] Ostrow explained how the clinic strong-armed the state-funded laboratories into testing their anonymous samples:

The city clinics and the state-operated health clinics got money from the [federal government] and they're obligated under those grants . . . to provide testing for any STD samples that came into them, whether they're from their own labs or from doctor's offices or hospitals or whatever. So we said, "We're going to send you samples, but you're not going to have names. You're just going to have a code by which we'll be able to identify who the person is, and we'll give you their zip code so you can . . . continue to keep statistics on rates of STDs by zip code but we're going to do the contact tracing."[15]

With this simple shift in procedure, the Howard Brown Memorial Clinic provided a sense of security for gay men as they came to the clinic and got tested. Furthermore, while the clinic informed patients of positive test results, it placed the onus of telling previous sexual partners of their disease(s) on the patients themselves, as opposed to city health workers or clinic staff. Through standardized anonymous testing, the Chicago clinic granted agency to their gay clients. At the Howard Brown clinic respectful and informed doctors, who trusted patients to notify previous and future partners of any diseases, anonymously tested gay men. These were all major changes for gay health care in Chicago, as, "prior to the clinic's founding, there was nowhere in Chicago a gay [man] could receive competent, confidential, and affordable healthcare for sexually transmitted diseases. Gay patients were occasionally subject to blackmail or overcharges, and frequently subject to disrespectful treatment in the form of contempt or "morality lectures."[16]

Employing free state testing of blood samples in new ways, gay health clinics served as a public health intermediary, providing test results from public laboratories while abandoning the actions and policies of public clinics that alienated gay patients. In these new gay health clinics, like the Howard Brown clinic, the Fenway clinic, and others, gay clients met welcoming (and increasingly knowledgeable) health-care providers who enacted new policies, mindful of the discretion many gay clients wanted. The universal and uncoordinated implementation of, at least optional if not universal, anonymous testing and self-contact tracing policies by gay health service providers across the country, including in Denver, Kansas City, Atlanta, Milwaukee, and Seattle, demonstrates the barrier to effective gay health services problematic public health contact-tracing policies posed. By deploying state resources, namely, the free testing of blood samples by state and federally funded laboratories, in new ways, gay health activists laid the foundation for themselves and for larger medical interventions in both the gay community and the larger medical profession. Meanwhile, despite the frustration of public health departments regarding the manipulation of their policies, the state unintentionally allowed for gay health activism to take root in the 1970s.

Regulatory Reckoning in Boston

Various state policies, regulations, and legal requirements also shaped gay health clinics across the country during the 1970s. The state played a major role in the creation of gay health clinics in a variety of ways. Local and federal redevelopment plans ignited health activism in the Fenway neighborhood, while the Los Angeles Gay Community Services Center founders adopted a strategically traditional organizational structure designed to win Internal Revenue Service (IRS) nonprofit status. The state remained a constant force in the development of these clinics throughout the decade through licensure processes, requirements for insurance, and taxes. As a result of this state involvement, clinics grappled with remaining true to their founding principles and activist ethos, that were often critical of or in direct opposition to the state, while also remaining open and serving their communities. Those that remained operational struck delicate balances that proved pragmatic yet fueled by activism.

After the battle with the Boston Redevelopment Authority (BRA) ended victoriously for neighborhood activists in 1973 with a legal ruling that demanded a neighborhood-elected board approve and aid in designing all development projects, the Fenway clinic's relationship with the state grew increasingly complex. On the one hand, the Fenway clinic became increasingly dependent on the state, at both the federal and the municipal levels, for funding, licensure, and inspection approvals to provide health services to its quickly growing number of patients. Complicating this growing dependence, both the federal and municipal governments became increasingly strict in regularly enforcing compliance with existing and newly created regulations before granting more funding and licensure. On the other hand, the policies and culture of the Fenway Community Health Clinic, which emanated from a distrust and dislike of the government's instigating and antagonizing role in the neighborhood's battle against redevelopment, focused more on providing services and creating community than on complying with government regulations. However, new regulations under the second Nixon administration requiring that clinics receiving federal funding meet building and licensure codes, use only trained and certified medical professionals, and comply with standard bookkeeping practices for billing and payroll called for massive changes in culture and protocol in some volunteer-run community clinics like the Fenway clinic.[17] In short, the politics of the Fenway Community Health Clinic grew progressively out of sync with the government's increasingly regulatory policies for community health clinics as the decade progressed.

Here the state acted as a hegemonic force, but in ways different than in previous generations, in which the state sought to make its citizens "straight" through various forms of legal violence.[18] Unlike the examples cited by Margot Canaday in her book *The Straight State,* such as the rejection of suspected gay immigrants at the border, compliance with these state regulations didn't preclude gay identity or activity, but instead demanded professional conformity and encouraged further enmeshment with the state. At first glance, this relationship to the state might appear benign, while in reality it usurped agency and power from gay activists and organizations in return for funding amounts that prevented systemic transformation of mainstream health services beyond the gay health clinic setting. The state still perpetrated legal violence, but in more insidious ways and with different aims. It appeared relatively ambivalent about whether the services offered allowed for the survival of individual sexual minorities or stronger communities among sexual minorities, as long as those people and groups were compliant, submissive, and "docile" to the state, to use Foucault's language.[19] From this vantage point, the state acted less as a straight state than as an antiqueer state—meaning it encouraged assimilation while quashing the possibility of structural transformation—a concept many scholars have traced in interactions between current political movements and the state, but have yet to apply to the 1970s.[20]

Despite the growing tension between the state's regulations and the clinic's ethos, the clinic thrived, seeing its patient numbers rise exponentially throughout the decade. The clinic was open five days a week, handling everything from cases of the flu and child immunizations to blood pressure checks and postoperative care.[21] Within two years of the opening of the Haviland

Street space, the Fenway clinic logged over five thousand patient visits.[22] The Gay Health Collective, by far the fastest-growing of the clinic's services, expanded to two nights a week by the middle of the decade.[23] However, in return for its continued growth, the clinic would soon be expected to conform and capitulate to the state's regulations and expectations.

This vibrancy resulted in part from the clinic's focus on providing care and building community among Fenway residents, which, at the time, translated into deprioritizing professional qualification for staff, standards for which were often set by the state or medical profession, which the clinic critiqued. To care for the ever-growing number of patients, the Fenway clinic drew from the ranks of nearby Harvard Medical School, Deaconess Hospital, and Brigham Women's Hospital. The clinic became a hot spot for medical students and residents. Excited to hone their medical skills while also serving the surrounding community, and often at an earlier point in their training than most clinics and hospitals allowed, "they were getting really good experience."[24] The volunteers at the Fenway Community Health Clinic were either passionate about the neighborhood or passionate about providing free health care to those who needed it. Just as community members literally built the clinic, despite their ignorance of building construction, they also ran it, despite limited community health know-how. Placing greater value on passion than on qualifications translated into having "some physicians on staff . . . who had not completed their training . . . nurses who had backgrounds that were not relevant . . . laboratory personnel who were chemistry majors in college but never had taken any chemical laboratory training."[25] The volunteers responsible for billing often had some bookkeeping experience but often "didn't know the first thing about really setting up medical billing and grant writing and the like."[26] Most volunteers worked only a handful of hours per week, so that single tasks often spread out across multiple volunteers, compounding these issues even more. Scondras remembered, "We had no particular group of people running the place, it was just a collective . . . if you showed up, you ran it."[27] Consequently, the more detailed and ongoing tasks like billing or building management fell between the cracks. This constantly changing cast of characters also made complying with government regulations both difficult and seemingly unimportant.

When not lost amid the bustle of the clinic, the Fenway clinic met the state's increased enforcement of regulations with resistance. In the eyes of

Figure 9. Staff and volunteers of the Fenway Community Health Center. Fenway Community Health Center records, 1972–2007, M172, box 10, folder 22, Northeastern University Archives, Boston.

Fenway residents, government policies at the federal, state, and municipal levels had contributed to the neighborhood's decline into poverty and eventually encouraged an army of wrecking balls. The resulting cynicism among Fenway residents was deep and lasting, so much so that the government's plan to better enforce regulations and impose professional standards at the community clinic engendered both frustration and renewed hostility toward the state. Scondras recalled getting a notice from the state regarding the clinic's noncompliance with licensure and the inspection code: "The state tried to clamp down on us because we didn't have a license to operate as a clinic. . . . I remember getting the letter and ripping it up. . . . They told us to stop, and we said no."[28] Furthermore, the defeat of the BRA gave Fenway activists greater certainty that the political backlash of attacking a community health clinic insulated the clinic from any real governmental threat. Scondras described their rationale: "They didn't want to kick us out, they didn't want to look like bad guys. . . . It was politically impossible to touch us."[29] During the BRA struggle, the clinic played a central role in successful political and publicity strategies to gain sympathy and support for the Fenway residents. Certainly, few local politicians publicly criticized the thriving clinic, just as few took issue with the Black Panther Clinic blocking another major city redevelopment project that had inspired Scondras and Beane to open the Fenway clinic. In fact the clinic welcomed Boston mayor Kevin White and many other local government officials to its official opening in 1973, even as the clinic was a clear and intentional threat to the city's redevelopment plans.[30] As a result of their perceived unassailable political position, the Fenway activists who knew of the regulations and requirements often chose to ignore them, or work around them. In fact, the clinic operated for seven years, until 1978, without obtaining its full licensure from the Massachusetts Department of Public Health.[31]

While able to skirt the "thankfully-slow-moving state bureaucracy" that enforced regulations, inspections, and state licensure, the clinic couldn't avoid its dwindling eligibility for funding without compliance.[32] Government grants for which the clinic, without major changes, was eligible became scarcer and less lucrative as regulations became increasingly common and strictly enforced over the decade. Instead the clinic focused on programs and grants for which it could easily qualify without licensure as a clinic, like family planning grants through Title IX programming, rat prevention grants through the city, and university-funded health research and outreach programs.[33] In 1976 the clinic teamed with the Department of Public Health to educate various communities, including gay men, about VD prevention and treatment.[34] A Tufts-based researcher offered to pay for Giardia testing for gay clients at the Fenway clinic who were willing to answer a medical questionnaire, thus allowing the clinic to offer the test to its clients starting in 1978.[35] These and similar relatively small and low-cost projects allowed the clinic access to more funding, but not of the size or magnitude it needed to avoid deficits. These smaller grants, in addition to the Deaconess match-grant that paid for some medical supplies and staffing, permitted the Fenway clinic to continue operating without significantly changing its political or organizational culture, though such grants did little to relieve the clinic's growing financial instability or put it more in step with the larger social and political trends of the decade.

In late 1979, facing patient numbers far outpacing revenue, the board hired a new executive director for the struggling Fenway clinic in the hope that the leadership change would bring about greater financial stability. With a history of health-care management and community projects, Sally Deane started her tenure as the executive director in January 1980 only to realize that the organization was on the brink of collapse. In addition to having "no written standards for employment, personnel policies, quality assurance standards, or management reports," the clinic required significant renovations before its inspection for licensure renewal, which was due to take place just three months after Deane's arrival.[36] However, the clinic's financial situation quickly became her greatest concern especially after "finding . . . signed checks made out to the . . . government for withholding taxes that had never been mailed because the checks would have bounced. . . . Even though they alleged that they were operating on a $200,000 budget with 7,000 patient visits, maybe 2,000 patients, they were technically in bankruptcy."[37] On her tenth day as the executive director, Deane learned that the clinic had not paid payroll taxes for quite some time and the IRS was on the verge of closing it down. The clinic's avoidance of professionalization and regulatory compliance had left it in great danger of losing its license, its funding, and shutting down completely.

Seeing no other option, Deane looked to longtime community partner Deaconess Hospital to give the Fenway clinic a loan to pay its back taxes. The decision marked the moment when clinic's trajectory changed. Before lending the needed money, the Deaconess required assurances of better business practices on the part of the clinic, in short, compliance with state regulations and guidelines. For Deane, promises to reform the more slapdash aspects of the clinic were easy, as she already had plans to codify new professional standards, implement billing practices, and streamline the decision-making process. One longtime volunteer remembered how she felt when the Fenway board agreed to accept the loan from Deaconess: "I thought it was a necessary thing to do, but I thought it was a sad necessary thing to do."[38] For many of the Fenway clinic community at large, the loan from Deaconess, and the professionalization it demanded, were bittersweet, allowing the clinic to remain open, but also demanding an end of the political culture and structure that defined the clinic. The state, this time in the form of back taxes, again proved incredibly influential in the evolution of the clinic.

In a vote that formally marked the end of the consensus and democratic days of the Fenway clinic, the board granted Deane much more oversight and control over policies and procedures at the clinic in an effort to expedite all the necessary changes demanded by the loan and required for the upcoming licensure inspection. With this new power, the immediate threat of closure behind her, and the IRS paid, Deane focused her attention on transforming the Fenway clinic into a more professional organization. First off, she "took a stand that the medical staff had to be qualified to do the work that they were doing."[39] Under these new policies, physicians had to be eligible for board certification in order to volunteer or work at the clinic, which meant "no more med students."[40] Nurses and laboratory technicians also had to have proper training and licensure. However, personnel was not the only issue as Deane struggled to bring the clinic up to code. She faced an inspection by the Massachusetts Department of Public Health in order to renew the clinic's license. While the previous generation of Fenway clinic staff had avoided licensure for many years, Deane saw maintaining the clinic's license as crucial to its future. After numerous renovations, paid for with money from Deaconess, the Fenway clinic passed government inspection and renewed its license in 1981. Going beyond the physical structure and the personnel within it, Deane, along with newly hired staff, instituted a new accounting system that "allowed for third party billing, including Medicaid and private insurers, making the financial base . . . more solid."[41] As a result of these major institutional changes, the Fenway Community Health Clinic went from evading and circumnavigating any form of organizational hierarchy and professionalization to embracing and epitomizing both—all within a year of Deane's hiring.

When the Fenway Community Health Clinic finally succumbed to the state's pressure to professionalize in the interest of becoming a financially and medically strong institution, Fenway neighborhood activists and the free health-care movement that had been at the clinic's core parted ways. Many neighborhood activists left the Fenway clinic shortly after the acceptance of the loan, falling victim to Deane's insistence on standards for employment. Volunteering and community involvement had been at the heart of the Fenway clinic and a crucial piece in making it so interwoven with the Fenway neighborhood as it battled the BRA. However, as a result of many of Deane's new policies, many staff and longtime volunteers were suddenly "unqualified" to do the jobs they had been doing, in some cases for years. One community member recalled how the transition influenced her decision to leave the board: "I quit the board because I didn't think I could make a contribution. . . .

There was nothing left for an ordinary citizen to do. I wasn't the right match for that board anymore." [42] Many volunteers and community members no longer felt welcome in the clinic that many had come to think of as a community center, a home away from home. However, even with the changes, the clinic maintained its commitment to free and low-cost quality health care.

Faced with extinction or evolution as a result of the state pressure to regulate, the clinic adapted to become pragmatic *and* idealistic and in this way held tight to both its commitment to low-cost care for underserved people and activist ideals. By the end of 1980, Deane's changes at the Fenway clinic had filtered into every aspect of the clinic. Its new structures and policies made for faster decision making, although it was more hierarchical and excluding of community members. Billing Medicare, Medicaid, and insurance companies was more consistent and reliable than ever before, and the clinic's financial situation slowly became more stable, shoring up its sliding fee scale. Before, this type of billing was intermittent and slapdash at best, meaning that the clinic's main sources of income were donations, sliding-scale fee payments, and the dwindling number of small grants for which the clinic was eligible. Creating a reliable and integrated billing method whereby the clinic actually made the most use of the various forms of insurance its clients had available provided stability, predictability, and increased cash flow for the clinic. Many gay clients still shied away from using their employee-based medical insurance for fear of their employers learning of their sexuality and firing them, but the funds brought in by the other clients and services helped support the gay services.

With its new professionalization, the clinic saw the number of grants for which it was eligible increase and had trained volunteers and staff applying for them. Again, the state appears ambivalent about whether the clinic directed services toward gay clients and more concerned about the clinic's response to the state's exertion of power through regulation, offering carrots and sticks accordingly. The Fenway clinic thrived, continuing to provide low-cost health care to underserved communities and thus remaining true to the counterculture politics of the neighborhood activists. The pressures and changes that occurred in the Fenway clinic in 1980 certainly signal the rise of a more politically and financially conservative period nationally, but they also showcase the resilience and adaptability of the New Left ideals. Weathering the various challenges posed by the state positioned the clinic to flourish in the 1980s and beyond, demonstrating again the state's often unintentional and unexpected role in the rise and maintenance of gay health services in the pre-AIDS era.

The State Political Wedge

The power of the state in the development and evolution of gay health services in the 1970s becomes even clearer through the lens of state and federal funding. State funds made clinic operations (at least partially) possible, but not without stipulations that often transformed the clinics, their ethos, and their relationship to the communities they served. Through funding that was often program specific and bound to numerous regulations, and that demanded grantees refrain from political work or rhetoric, the state proved particularly adept at driving a wedge between clinic services and the radical politics that had sparked their creation. Thus, the state both enabled the growth of gay health services and dictated their political and institutional trajectory.

In Los Angeles, the cracks in this relationship between services and politics began to surface very shortly after the founders of the Gay Community Services Center opted for a conventional organizational structure as a means to gain tax-exempt status and potential funding. For the radical faction within the center, which blended the politics of gay liberation, feminism, the Black Panthers, the Brown Berets, labor, and other radical political groups of the time, accepting state funding posed a series of problems. First, they argued philosophically that, by accepting state funding, founders and management became extensions of the state. They viewed state funding, and the requisite prudence on the part of management, as in direct contradiction to the radical liberation politics that they saw at the core of the center's founding. From their perspective, the acceptance of state funds was tantamount to introducing and reinforcing within the center many forms of oppression radicals commonly associated with the government and mainstream society. One handout by the center's radical contingent argued, "Boss Imposed, Patriarchial [sic], Racist, Classist Control Of Lesbian And Gay Programs Is NO SERVICE to Lesbian Women and Gay Men: THE U.S. GOVERNMENT GIVES US THAT MUCH!"[43] Many of these critiques highlighted tensions already present within the center, evidenced by lesbians' early frustration with sexism among gay men at the center.[44] However, government funding and the concomitant move away from a more militant and liberationist politics by center founders and management created a nearly catastrophic ideological chasm between the state and center on one side and center volunteers and activists on the other.

In addition to their concern over the center's philosophical complicity with state-supported oppression, the activists pointed to examples of it in practice within the center in the state funding of particular programs. Starting in 1973, the vast majority of funding at the Los Angeles Gay Community Services Center came from some level of the government, with most monies awarded to specific programs within the center rather than to the center as a whole.[45] The center's resources became concentrated in a handful of programs that often serviced small subsets of the gay community, and excluded factions saw the resulting financial disparities between programs and groups as proof of the center's political shift away from radicalism and its increasing institutional sexism, classism, and racism. A press release entitled "'Gay Center' Shafts Gays!" written in April 1973 by members of a housing collective who lived in a building owned by the center and located next door shed light on how program development and funding fueled early divisions within the center. In 1973, the center obtained a federal grant to transform the building that housed the collective into a rehabilitation center for gays and lesbians with drug- and alcohol-abuse issues. In response to their concomitant eviction, housing collective members accused the center, specifically Kight and Kilhefner, of being sexist, racist, corrupt, manipulative, and responsible for religious and political persecution.[46] The housing collective members went so far as to suggest that the center created the drug- and alcohol-abuse program to garner support from the larger gay and lesbian community and simultaneously divert attention from the eviction of "gay brothers and sisters who are not in a position, by virtue of their life-style, to gain the Center heavy Federal and Foundation funding."[47] While the housing collective's accusations were some of the most extreme during the early years of the center, they illustrate how growing resentment among some over the center's use of government funding blossomed into a full-blown critique of the center's abandonment of radical politics.

State funding regulations seemed particularly, if unintentionally, deft at exacerbating existing tensions within the Gay Community Services Center, especially those between lesbians and gay men. Specific provisions in state and federal funding designed to suppress discrimination toward oppressed groups ironically translated into the biggest challenge for lesbian health services at the center. As a result of various pieces of legislation, including the Civil Rights Act of 1964, government funds granted to the center forbade partisan activity, affiliation, preference, or bias for a specific group or minority.[48] This provision meant that the center could not show preference for gays and lesbians either by denying services to heterosexuals or by encouraging homosexuality, fueling frustration among radical activists within the center.[49] As lesbians struggled to create programmatic parity after the center subsumed the Gay Women's Service Center, Lisa Meyer and Sharon Raphael set their sights on creating a lesbian health clinic to mirror the gay men's health clinic. The free Women's Clinic opened in February 1973. To cover operating costs, the Women's Clinic applied for and accepted a $10,000 family planning grant from the Los Angeles Regional Family Planning Council that year. In accordance with nondiscrimination provisions, the grant required the lesbian clinic to publicize itself in the surrounding neighborhood as a free clinic and offer its services to the larger community. Meyer recalled that "within minutes" of receiving the grant and publicizing the clinic, "the waiting room was full of mom and dad and six kids lined up for these free services."[50] The clinic's sudden popularity among a mostly straight population had major implications for the staff, many of whom worked with the heterosexual population in their workplaces and volunteered at the center specifically to work with the lesbian community. Meyer explained that "within a matter of a very short time, like a month or six weeks, [the volunteer doctor] quit and the nurses quit and the techs quit. Everybody quit. . . . They were doing this out of the kindness of their hearts to serve the lesbian community."[51] The actual clinic clientele consisted of disproportionately more racial minorities, specifically Latinos, than what the clinic founders and volunteers, many of whom were racial minorities themselves, had anticipated when setting out to serve the city's lesbians. However, issues with sexuality, not race, drove the volunteer exodus. Many lesbians found a waiting room filled with heterosexual women and some accompanying men unappealing and unwelcoming. Even more problematically, staffing the clinic became a major struggle. The clinic closed within a matter of months and failed to thrive in numerous later iterations throughout the decade.[52]

The apolitical stipulations of government funding that had compromised the success of the free Women's Clinic riled radicals throughout the center. Even though government funding was generally program specific, it came with stipulations that had an impact on the entire center, meaning that if any center program accepted government funding, no center program could appear overtly political or preferential to gays or lesbians. At the Los Angeles Gay Community Services Center's founding, Kight, Kilhefner, and Platania placed politicized health, specifically the concept of oppression sickness, as an ideological and programmatic cornerstone for the center. With the oppression sickness model, every service for gays and lesbians challenged their oppression and consequently treated the sickness born out of their oppression. From this perspective, every service was a health program, and every program aided in the liberation of gays and lesbians from their political oppression within a heterosexist society. In short, oppression sickness used health as a political tool, and politics infused every service at the center. This understanding of health resonated with the radical politics of the founders themselves and the radical activists within the gay and lesbian community. Yet, it stood in clear opposition to the state's demand that organizations granted nonprofit status remain apolitical. As the center sought nonprofit status from the IRS from the outset and then pursued state funding, it always downplayed its official ties to this political framing, hoping to *appear* apolitical on paper but *be* political in reality.

The realities of this political disconnect came to a head in 1975, when, after much lobbying and many applications on the part of volunteers, the center was awarded a $1 million grant that would be disseminated over three years for a women's alcoholism project in the spring of 1975.[53] The program would provide the most comprehensive free and voluntary intensive counseling and rehabilitation services to women with alcohol-abuse issues in the city. However, upon announcement of the award the center declared itself "ill-equipped to staff" and manage such a large grant and came to the conclusion that "the Women's Alcohol Program of the Gay Community Services Center has not been inter-faced with the total program of the Center, as conceptualized, and that seemingly it cannot be within the current intellectual climate of that Program and its Staff."[54] The women who had spearheaded the creation of the Women's Alcohol Program opted to leave the Gay Community Services Center and form their own separate organization with the grant. Yet, the center's fumbling of the grant because of their relatively undeveloped oversight and organizational capabilities proved the final straw for disgruntled workers and volunteers, many of whom were among the radical faction within the center and had long been frustrated with the widening gap between the center's oppression sickness rhetoric and actual practices. Many lesbian staff, volunteers, and community members interpreted the failure of the grant—which would have been the largest grant received to date by the Gay Community Services Center and would have made the center's largest program one solely for women—as yet another example of women being treated unfairly by the male-dominated center.[55] A number of women in leadership roles also decided to leave their positions, and the center altogether, to oversee the Women's Alcohol Program as it became its own entity, feeding the radical and feminist critique of the bungled grant and the center.[56] From the radical viewpoint, the botched grant illustrated the center's betrayal of radicalism on two counts: through its affiliation with government funding and its reinforcement of sexism through its mishandling of the grant.

The failure of the Women's Alcohol Program in the early months of 1975 brought the tensions over the center's shifting politics and its relationship to the state to a climax. From the perspective of the radical faction within the center, the poor handling of the grant illustrated the ways in which the center's organizational structure, management, and dependence on state funding contributed to the institution's sexism, economic inequality, racism, and political oppression of radical and militant gays and lesbians. Though the state demanded apolitical services and set the terms for funding programs, the radicals within the center set their sights on those they saw as directly responsible for the center's relationship to the state and resulting politics: the founders, board of directors, and management. In early April 1975 an in-house newsletter entitled "It's About Time" began circulating within the center and larger gay and lesbian communities.[57] Revealing the multidimensionality of the radical analysis of the center's shifting politics, they explained their purpose:

[We] stand against male control of women, and boss control of workers, no matter how subtle. We oppose patriarchal forms of structure (such as the "boss" imposed Management Team and the absentee landlordship of our Board of Directors) which foster alienation among those who are committed to social change and the growth of our community . . . our purpose is to focus upon and create a feminist identity here at GCSC. We seek this goal because we are committed to a non-sexist and non-classist working environment.[58]

The authors of "It's About Time" were not angry with just one policy or aspect of the center. Rather, they challenged the entirety of the organization's policies, decision making, and funding process, arguing that the institutional culture that resulted from all of these was sexist, classist, racist, and smothering to all forms of political radicalism. This problematic institutional culture could be traced back to and was exacerbated by the center's decision to seek state approval and funding and to appear conventional from its founding. The newsletter outlined the exclusion of women and center workers and volunteers in the current two-part organizational structure. The board of directors in 1975 had six male members, one female, and two vacancies. Meanwhile the management team, imagined at its founding as a six-person team, consisted only of founders Morris Kight and Don Kilhefner at the time.[59] The six-page handout also made clear their perspective on the relationship between government funding and the problems of the center: "With the first acceptance of outside funding . . . the Gay Community Services Center drastically altered the philosophy and direction of the Center."[60] The articles in the newsletter then went on to trace how the funding and founders were at the root of the center's oppressive hierarchy and policies. "It's About Time" shed light on the gap between the politics of the radical faction within the center and those of the larger organization in a way and with an intensity never before seen.

The response elicited by the newsletter was also unprecedented and strongly influenced by the state. As the newsletter spread throughout the center and out into the larger Los Angeles community, Kight, Kilhefner, and other board members grew concerned that the center would lose not only its state funding but also its tax-exempt status because of the highly politicized rhetoric and charges put forth by the "It's About Time" authors. A memorandum dated April 21 and sent to all center staff and volunteers explained that all county funding contracts would "be held in suspension."[61] In an effort to avoid any permanent damage to their funding relationships the memo went on to threaten termination unless "workers of the Gay Community Service Center, agree [to]. . . . not use public funds. . . . for political purposes. . . . not use time paid for by public funds (which includes donations) for political activities. . . . and not use public funds (which includes donations) whether salaries, supplies, equipment, etc. for the purpose of attacking the GCSC Board of Directors, the management structure and/or funding sources in public ways and in the media."[62] Enraged by the demands of the memo, dubbed by some a "loyalty oath" again illustrating how radicals portrayed the Center as an extension of an oppressive state, on April 24, a larger group of radicals from within the center presented the board of directors and the management team with a long list of concerns about the center's financial management and management's treatment of center workers and volunteers. Along with the detailed list of complaints, twenty-one workers signed a demand for the dismissal of the fiscal officer, the director of program development, and the board of directors.[63] The group's focus on these specific positions illustrates the clear relationship the radical faction felt existed between the center's funding and program policies (which aligned with state grant requirements) and its political shift. When the management team and board of directors refused this demand, the group took their concerns directly to the organizations that provided funding to the center, including the state and federal governments.[64]

By contacting local, state, and federal funders directly with their complaints about center management, the radicals hoped to both portray existing management as ineffective and show that the center was far more radical than previously thought by funding agencies, making the center unworthy of government funding. By contacting the funders, the radicals within the center effectively threatened to shut it down, potentially permanently, all in an effort to transform the center into a truly radical organization in which oppression in any form was not acceptable and politics were not compromised for or by funding. The state flexed its muscle in its initial response, freezing all payments to the center and suspending all contracts until the crisis was resolved. In doing so, the state forced center management and the board of directors to once again choose between its funding and its politics. They could either step down, resigning the center to the radical contingent's leadership, which would certainly translate into a loss of funding and potentially the end of the center, or they could recommit to state funding requirements and distance themselves further from their politically radical roots. Within hours of the meeting on April 24, Kight presented the board with a proposal for a nineteen-step response, including "that we make up a team of Board members and Management Team, to visit with each of the [funding] agencies to clarify our status, to re-assure them of our commitment."[65] The board adopted the proposal, and the center successfully mended relationships with all its funding sources within the following weeks.

Repairing the relationship with the state at the local, state, and federal levels required more than simple face-to-face placations; the center also had to address the internal strife at the root of the crisis. On May 1, after "a marathon six day meeting" the board of directors fired eleven workers including all of the contributors to "It's About Time."[66] The board gave each of the released workers reasons for their firing that related to their job performance, and informed many that "your association with 'It's About Time' and those in support of it, and other such activities, has, we believe, placed our charter, our tax exempt status, and our public funding in jeopardy."[67] In firing the most radical and vocal dissenters within the center, management once again committed to their institutional vision "to be the Corporate Body so desperately needed in a large agency such as the Center, holding enormous public funding, and with a crucially needed, though now badly blunted, multi-purpose, co-sexual, inclusive and comprehensive program for all women and men who seek us out."[68] Here the center also demonstrated its allegiance to the state and its associated funding over radical politics, again illustrating the way in which the state functioned less as a "straight state" and more as an antiqueer state. In short, by firing the most politically outspoken at the center, the center management and board made a pragmatic, if difficult, decision to provide social services to the gay and lesbian communities rather than to embody the more idealistic politically radical vision of the 1960s and early 1970s to which the fired radicals still clung. The center also showed very transparently how the state had reshaped its politics—a development that the founding proposal for the center seemed to predict while simultaneously attempting to embrace the radical politics of the local context.

For those fired, the self-described "Feminist 11," the board's actions only showed both how in line with the state and consequently how destructive the center had become to radical gay and lesbian politics. They were a racially diverse group of five men and six women who came from a wide range of the center's program offerings, including the women's health clinic, the men's VD clinic, the counseling services, the hotline, and the third-world awareness program. Jeanne Cordova, board member and full-time staff publicist for the women's health clinic, became the loudest voice of those fired by the center.[69] By 1975 Cordova had earned a reputation as a key lesbian activist in Los Angeles. She began her activism serving as president of the Los Angeles chapter of Daughters of Bilitis at the start of the decade and then left to found the Los Angeles Lesbian Center and the nationally disseminated *Lesbian Tide* news magazine, both in 1971. As publisher of the *Lesbian Tide*, Cordova posed the greatest public relations problem for the center after she left, as she used the news magazine to rally support for those fired and to vilify the Gay Community Services Center. Using the *Lesbian Tide* as their political bullhorn, the fired workers immediately set up a picket line and called for all Gay Community Services Center employees and patrons to strike.[70] In addition to editorials and articles in the *Lesbian Tide*, the Feminist 11 engaged in an all-out battle with their former employer as they "leafleted heavily, held a community meeting . . . , appeared before community groups . . . , [and] published various materials."[71] In each of these forums the rhetoric employed by the Feminist 11 and their supporters became increasingly personal as it portrayed the firings as a direct result of the classism and sexism of the individuals on the management team and the members of the board of directors. To this end, protesters picketed not only the center but also the homes and workplaces of board members.[72] Their goal was clear: to turn public opinion against the center in an effort to force either the management to leave or the center to shut down.

The picket line, while relatively small, came to include the rhetoric of and activists from many of the radical political groups within the larger Los Angeles gay and lesbian communities.[73] The larger lesbian feminist community as well as gay male feminists, like the five men in the Feminist 11, sympathized with the strikers on the basis of the center's apparent sexism. Members of the gay communist group Lavender and Red Union mobilized around the unfair treatment of the fired center workers.[74] Also, as the Feminist 11 consisted of some of the most outspoken advocates for people of color within the center, many gays and lesbians of color supported the strike to protest the center's apparent racism.[75] While each group brought its own political interests to the strike, the Feminist 11 created a unified coalition among the radicals of the gay and lesbian community. In an era known for the fracturing of the radical Left along the lines of identity, the supporters of the Feminist 11 offer a contrasting example of collaboration and integration of radicals of many different stripes within the gay community. But even with a broad base of support from numerous groups within the gay and lesbian community, the actual size of the coalition in terms of numbers was relatively small, and the picket line rarely consisted of more than twenty people.[76]

While it unified the diminishing radical factions within the gay and lesbian communities, the strike cemented the relationship between the center and the state as much as it made permanent the split in the center between social services and radical politics. The Feminist 11 portrayed the center staff and management as "male-identified bourgeois capitalist sexist lackey pigs."[77] Meanwhile, the board of directors began to attack the Feminist 11, depicting them as selfish, rigid ideologues whose own narrow politics placed the center's very existence at risk and whose tactics of "beating on windows . . . spitting on Center Board members . . . threatening to burn the building down . . . letting out the air of staff persons tires" were dangerous and sophomoric.[78] By the end of May the Feminist 11 and the Gay Community Services Center had traded lawsuits with one another. The Gay Community Services Center filed a restraining order against the Feminist 11, while the Feminist 11 sued their former employer for wages and other concessions.[79]

These lawsuits, and the strike, were finally settled in 1978, but the separation between social services and radical politics would remain permanent at the center. Ultimately, the Los Angeles Gay Community Services Center conceded publicly that the Feminist 11 had been unfairly terminated and agreed to pay "token reparations."[80] For the board members and the remaining staff, the strike shed light on the fact that the center was "undermanaged and unprepared for the transition from a period of being totally a volunteer agency to an agency with government funding needing to be accountable and responsible."[81] Consequently, to address many of the individual work-related grievances of radicals and to provide a structure that allowed for easier growth, the center revised its personnel policies and procedures, providing clarity to both worker grievance and termination procedures, and underwent a formal audit of all its finances.[82] Each of these actions also made the center even more appealing to state funding agencies. By the time the agreement was finalized in 1978, "in a spirit of reconciliation, the Center share[d] strong desires with the strikers and their supporters to lay this issue at rest."[83] There was certainly fatigue on both sides of the picket line.

Despite the challenges posed by the strike, the Gay Community Services Center had continued to grow in terms of funding, programs, and visitors after an initial falloff immediately following the crisis. By 1976, the center consisted of three buildings: one for a temporary residential program for gay parolees, another for the center's residential rehabilitation program, and the third housing the actual center. In addition, the center offered a wide and growing set of more than two dozen services ranging from health clinics to rap groups, and from job training and placement programs to a secondhand store.[84] In 1975 the center served over a thousand people. The demographics of the center's patrons show that it attracted people of nearly every age and race with roughly 40 percent of service recipients being female.[85] By 1978, the men's VD clinic alone accounted for more than 15,000 visits annually to the center.[86] While the strike created many immediate challenges for the center, clearly it had recovered and thrived with state support in the absence of the radicals.

State funding requirements and the struggles that emanated from them transformed the center in terms of size, budget, and services but also in terms of how it defined health. State funding stipulations forced the replacement of the umbrella concept of oppression sickness with more rigid and narrow definitions of health and health services. As, over time, the center became more dependent on state funding, it slowly adopted the state's definition of health as services directly related to physical or mental health. The center did not stop offering and expanding those services that fell outside the new definition of health, but instead abandoned the once potent political framing of oppression sickness. Consequently, the center found state funding for nonhealth programs as well, including a recurring Comprehensive Employment and Training Act grant for center worker training and employment and money from the Department of Housing and Urban Development that allowed the center to pay off its mortgage.[87] All of these grants shaped the center's new definition of health programs to be more in line with the definition used by the state, separating health from politics. By decade's end, at the state's insistence, the Los Angeles Gay Community Services Center had divorced all social services, including health programs, entirely from liberation politics.

The state proved a dynamic force in the creation and evolution of gay health services in the 1970s. It was an important accessory to the larger unwelcoming medical landscape that made gay health services necessary. The simple act of consistently pushing gay patients outside existing medical services, even as sexual norms shifted, laid the political foundation for gay health services across the country. The state also pulled gay health services into being by undergirding the services through mandated free blood sample testing. Throughout the decade, the state in all its iterations continued to shape gay health services, exerting increasing regulatory and funding force. As a result, many smaller clinics across the country shuttered, sometimes after just a few weeks of operation, when they either could not or would not comply with state regulations. Through regulatory compliance and increased opportunities for funding, the state molded those clinics that remained functioning, including the Fenway Community Health Clinic, the Howard Brown Memorial Clinic, and the Los Angeles Gay Community Services Center, into more professional institutions increasingly devoid of political rhetoric or programming. The state proved a strong force that demanded that gay health clinics become "more of an institution and less of a group of people that came together to do something."[88] Political radicalism consistently proved the victim in that transformation, suggesting the state in the 1970s was more antiqueer than straight. Exploring the evolution of gay health services and their relationship to and with the state in each of these cases suggests that the state—at the local, state, and federal levels—played an important, often unintentional, and stabilizing role in gay health services throughout the decade.

Despite the state's many methods of power and control in the development of gay health services, it did not completely undercut the agency of gay health activists or their patients. Activists themselves manipulated state policies and services to expand health-care offerings to a group that was traditionally underserved and often discriminated against. They circumvented standard public health reporting policies—a move that resulted in greater trust and health for gay patients. They also continued to make well-informed and measured decisions as their organizations became more, or less, enmeshed with the state, with some opting to close their clinics and advocate for gay health care in other ways, while others worked with the state in order to continue providing gay health services. Consequently, though the state had a significant impact on gay health services, activists and clinics remained true to their most basic goal: to increase access to quality medical care for gay patients. This included opening clinics, conducting research, educating existing health-care providers, doing outreach to skeptical communities, and building new, productive public health relationships. In short, providing quality health care to gay patients meant completely recasting the relationship between gay communities and medicine, and the state proved a necessary, if sometimes manipulative, unwitting, or reluctant, partner.

CHAPTER 4

REDEFINING GAY HEALTH

Despite gay health activists' varied political influences, their complex relationships with the state, and the shift toward conservatism of the political landscape, challenging notions of gay health lay at the very center of their activism. Whether framed as a form of political liberation, gay institution building, or reapplication of state resources to benefit a group historically ostracized, gay health activism required a renegotiation of the very meaning of gay health in both the medical and the gay communities. Stripped down to its essence, all gay health activism of the 1970s sought to challenge perceived gay sickness. Negotiations with local politics, activists, and the state also served as vehicles to reformulate understandings of health. Just as each clinic proved distinctive in its relationship to gay liberation, its political underpinnings, and its interaction with the state, each also approached the project of redefining gay health and sickness from a different position, often reflecting its idiosyncratic past. The end objective of a newly defined gay health that included easy access to welcoming, competent, and research-supported medical care for all gay patients generated a rich panoply of tactics that all worked toward this goal.

Gay health activists found new and increasingly effective ways to interact with both the larger gay population and the mainstream medical profession, challenging each to reinvent their understandings of sexual health and of each other. At the start of the decade, the practices of both gay patients and mainstream medical practitioners only amplified the skepticism each group had toward the other and exacerbated the effect of the VD epidemic on gay communities. However, the efforts of various gay health activists operating in multiple venues and in myriad capacities resulted in greater understanding and increased trust between many gay patients and mainstream medicine. This burgeoning and multifaceted trust proved the driving force behind shifting definitions of gay health in the 1970s.

Buying In to Community Health

Building trust among gay patients began by simply offering accurate, non-judgmental, low-cost, and gay-friendly services. As word spread of competent and courteous care, gay patients flocked to clinics, trust began to take root, and clinics scrambled to maintain quality services amid tremendous growth. All gay health activists across the country understood the need for these services, but none seemed prepared for the sheer number of gay patients in need. Furthermore, the vast majority of gay health activists in the early 1970s lacked the clinical experience to fully understand all that offering health services required. Chicago's David Ostrow, arguably one of the gay activists with the strongest medical and clinical background at the time, recalled that when the Howard Brown Memorial Clinic opened, "we had no money, we had no idea what we were getting ourselves into, we had *no* idea of the malpractice implications or we probably never would have done it."[1]

Ostrow and others at the Howard Brown Memorial Clinic quickly realized that they would need to be as reliant on the gay patients they served as those patients were on them for quality care. A crisis surrounding the clinic's malpractice insurance put this need for mutual trust and investment in sharp focus. Despite the casual nature of the formation and operation of the clinic, it still had to meet certain state and city requirements, which included maintaining malpractice insurance. Originally, the clinic operated under the license and malpractice insurance of Dr. Stanley Wissner, a University of Chicago–affiliated colleague of David Ostrow. As the clinic grew, patient numbers swelled, and volunteers became more numerous. Wissner's malpractice insurance became more costly and more restricted by the insurance company as it tried to protect itself from hefty malpractice settlements. Ostrow explained, "We had grown tremendously, and the doctors who volunteered with us, we were paying them to get supplemental riders to their own malpractice to cover their work at the clinic. But the volume was getting to such a point, I mean it grew exponentially."[2] In 1976, with the support of recent state legislation, the few insurance companies in Illinois that offered medical malpractice insurance banded together and decided to stop providing supplemental riders like the one Howard Brown Memorial Clinic depended on for coverage.[3] Consequently, the clinic had to get its own malpractice insurance at a cost of $10,000, more than doubling what it had been paying out to individual doctors to cover the supplemental rider fees.[4] Just two years after its birth, the clinic thus faced a malpractice insurance crisis and found itself on the brink of closure.

The outlook was bleak, as Ostrow attested: "$10,000 was more money than we had ever seen and was certainly more money than any organization, gay organization, had raised in the city at any one time."[5] For help, the clinic turned to relationships with gay businesses and the communities it had built over the last two years through its clinical work and the VD van program. In response to the plea for help, a number of Chicago bar owners and community activists organized a fund-raising event called the "Winter Carnival." The Lincoln Park Lagooners, a gay social and fund-raising group, hosted the event, while gay bars and businesses, all of which had participated in the VD van program at least once, sponsored the fund-raiser. The Sunday night event at the Aragon Theatre, a large concert venue in the city's Uptown neighborhood, attracted four thousand attendees, the largest gay event in the city at that time aside from a Pride parade.[6] By night's end, the Winter Carnival had raised $20,000, double the cost of the malpractice insurance premium.

While much of the advertising had focused on the Howard Brown Memorial Clinic's malpractice crisis, because the clinic was still a program of the umbrella organization Gay Horizons, all the proceeds from the Winter Carnival went to Gay Horizons. Gay Horizons made clear and gained approval from all involved in the event's initial planning that it planned to split the proceeds among its many programs, with the clinic getting only enough to cover the malpractice insurance. However, as the deadline for the malpractice insurance neared, Ostrow and others were shocked to learn that the director of Gay Horizons, a man named Bill Crick, without the approval of the Gay Horizons board or the board of the VD clinic, had chosen to spend all the raised money on a down payment for new community center instead.[7] Upon learning of the unauthorized purchase and the resulting inevitable closure of the clinic, many were outraged. The frustration stemmed not only from a feeling of having been deceived on the part of those who had organized the Winter Carnival and contributed to the cause, but also from loyalty to the clinic. Ostrow remembered the response to the news of Crick's move: "It was a huge melee that broke out at the meeting. Fortunately there was no physical violence."[8]

Many gay men across the city had become not only trusting of the Howard Brown clinic, but also invested in its success, a significant departure from their previous avoidance of all medical settings. Under intense pressure, the board of Gay Horizons voted to fire Bill Crick for having acted without their approval. They nullified Crick's attempts to purchase property for the organization and, having gotten the deposit returned, split the Winter Carnival proceeds according to the original agreement.[9] However, for Ostrow and others in the Howard Brown Memorial Clinic, the actions of Gay Horizons had done irreparable damage to their already strained and increasingly incompatible working relationship—they wanted to become their own, entirely separate organization.[10] The board of Gay Horizons agreed, voting to allow the clinic to become its own entity.[11] As a stand-alone clinic, Howard Brown continued to offer free VD testing Tuesday and Thursday nights out of the La Plaza office, strengthened and expanded the VD van program, and built an even stronger relationship with the gay businesses and communities that had saved it from financial ruin.[12] Patient numbers grew exponentially, from roughly 50 patients a month in 1974 to over 1,200 by 1980.[13] Immediately following the Winter Carnival and the clinic's split from Gay Horizons, the clinic initiated a continuous major capital improvement fund-raising program that resulted in tens of thousands of dollars for the clinic by the end of the decade.[14]

By offering gay-friendly health services, the Howard Brown Memorial Clinic challenged the widely held perception among gay patients and communities that all doctor's offices posed threats to gay men. While gay-friendly health services remained an anomaly within the medical mainstream, Howard Brown's offerings were enough to make gay patients and communities invest in the clinic's success and incorporate visits to the gay-friendly clinic into their understanding of gay health. While sparking a meaningful and drastic shift from the previous role a clinical setting played in community understandings of gay health, the clinic did not impact all gay communities' standards of gay health uniformly.

The Howard Brown Memorial Clinic remained on Chicago's historically white-majority North Side and directed most of its outreach programs, including the VD van, to bars and businesses with predominantly white patrons. While the clinic regularly employed rhetoric of inclusion for racial minorities and welcomed all its patients, it failed to employ practices and programs that translated into a strong patient base among racial minorities or among South or West Side gay residents.[15] Thus, as trust of the clinic took root in gay communities, signified in part by those communities' political and financial investment in the clinic, it appears to have been disproportionately from white gay North-Siders. Racial statistics for bar and bathhouse patrons and for gay social and fund-raising groups like the Lincoln Park Lagooners that spearheaded the initial and ongoing fund-raising for the Howard Brown Memorial Clinic do not exist. However, both historical accounts and the racial demographics of the neighborhoods in which these places and groups operated suggest that gay white men on the city's North Side experienced the greatest shift in their understandings of gay health as a direct result of the services of the Howard Brown Memorial Clinic. Even as the impact of the clinic's offerings fell unevenly across the city's gay communities, the shift in some communities' understanding of gay health to include mainstream medical intervention resulted in record-breaking numbers of VD diagnoses and treatments among gay men in the city.[16]

Becoming Gay

Redefining gay health for both the gay and the medical communities required an investment of money, time, and trust by gay patients, as in Chicago, as well as by service providers, as in the Fenway neighborhood in Boston. The interdependence between gay health service providers and their patients proved equally central in Boston, though it required much more from the Fenway clinic than from its patients. After the hiring of Executive Director Sally Deane and the settling of back taxes at the turn of the decade, the Fenway clinic also underwent a strategic-planning process designed to identify how the Fenway Community Health Clinic could have the greatest, most stabilizing, and sustained impact as a clinic while cutting unused or underused services that other area clinics made redundant. As part of the four-month strategic planning, the clinic collected information on the services of other area clinics, surveyed their patients, and assessed each of their programs. The main recommendation of the strategic-planning process was clear: the Fenway Community Health Clinic needed to become a clinic focused predominantly on serving Boston's gay and lesbian communities. To implement this recommendation, the clinic had to better understand the needs of gay and lesbian patients, address its homophobia as an organization, and trust its gay and lesbian patients to maintain and grow the clinic.

The Fenway clinic's historic indifference to gay liberation politics made the recommendation of the strategic-planning process unexpected. With few other providers of quality health services for gays and lesbians available throughout the 1970s, little doubt existed among certain gay communities that the Fenway clinic was the clinic for them, "a gay institution," as one 1978 article in the *Gay Community News* described it.[17] However, there was no confusion among clinic founders, volunteers, and staff that the clinic was a neighborhood clinic, not a gay one. This distinction informed not only the diverse services of the clinic, but the experiences of the gays and lesbians who worked there, offering insight into a closeted or gay ally organization rather than a fully out gay organization of the period. Sally Deane remembered that in preparation for her interview for the executive director position at the Fenway clinic in late 1979, "friends had advised me not to share with the search committee of the Board that I was gay, even though several members of the Board were gay. . . . These people were on the board because they cared about the services but not because they were gay political activists."[18] Those volunteers who maintained the Gay Health Collective were more likely to be out and politically active in gay communities, as in the case of Ron Vachon, yet their work within the clinic focused on the politics of health care rather than on gay liberation.[19] Clearly their work in providing gay health services was at some level an outgrowth of gay liberation in that gay liberation allowed for the clinic to publicize its services in gay newspapers, attract out gay doctors and medical professionals to volunteer their time, and of course, serve patients who benefited from, if they did not identify with, gay liberation. However, few of the staff and volunteers at the Fenway clinic saw themselves as gay liberation activists, whereas the larger gay community saw the clinic as providing vital services for the burgeoning gay community.[20] In short, many Boston gay patients considered the Fenway clinic an important part of their gay health, but the clinic defined health narrowly so as to include only medical services, rather than additional support or social services that would have fallen under the broader definition of health at work in Los Angeles, for example.

Though the strategic plan's recommendation for the Fenway clinic to focus on gay and lesbian health care surprised both gay patients and the clinic itself, when framed within the larger community health and political context of the city, the advice made sense. As the 1970s progressed, coalitions between movements and diverse groups gave way to identity-based services.[21] Just as Boston's gay offerings flourished and became synonymous with a more insular and predominantly white community concentrated in the area around the Boston Common over the decade, other groups also began to separate them-selves both physically and politically, with feminists rallying in Cambridge and blacks in Roxbury. As these groups created their own health organiza-tions, community clinics like the Fenway clinic saw their services become increasingly redundant.[22] The abundance of identity-based services forced the Fenway clinic to specialize its services as well. As the Fenway clinic's strategic planning process sought out ways to ensure the clinic's sustainability, its ser-vices to gay clients emerged as its strongest option for growth for three rea-sons. First, gay communities were growing quickly and steadily in this identity-based political atmosphere. Second, the Fenway clinic was the only area clinic to offer gay-friendly physical health services. Third, the number of clients at gay health nights grew consistently throughout the second half of the 1970s, a sign of the shifting definition of gay health within the city's gay communities.[23] In this way, the expansion of identity-based politics and ser-vices forced the Fenway clinic to abandon its broad service offerings and si-multaneously created a community that previously had little access to identity-specific services. Even as this reasoning was convincing, the recom-mendation to become a predominantly gay and lesbian clinic raised concerns for the board. Some, Deane among them, saw the proposed change as neces-sary, not because of an allegiance to gay communities or to gay liberation politics, but rather in the hope of ensuring the clinic's survival.[24]

There was great concern about creating tension with the neighborhood the clinic had been so influential in building, especially as the gay clientele of the Fenway clinic were much more white and middle class than many of the neighborhood residents. One *Gay Community News* piece highlighted the whiteness of Fenway's gay clients when it asked, "The gay night at Fenway

Health Center . . . where are the black faggots and lesbians, the Hispanics and other minorities?"[25] While the clinic at large offered its services to everyone and had a racially and economically diverse clientele generally, white and middle-class men made up an increasing percentage of the patients seen specifically by the Gay Health Collective in the late 1970s. This homogenization of gay health consumers reflected two larger structural problems: the social and political conflation of gay identity as a white identity in the 1970s and Fenway clinic's failure to specifically target gay communities of color with its outreach and services, making it complicit in the construction of gay as inherently white.

Beyond being concerned about the clinic's neighbors, critical board members were also concerned about the clinic and themselves. Over the 1970s, many of Boston's gay organizations had been the target of violence and vandalism, ranging from a fire at the Other Side bar to repeated break-ins at the *Gay Community News* offices.[26] Combined with regular acts of violence against gays in nearby Fens Park, the fears of violence and vandalism against a gay-identified clinic were legitimate.[27] Some individual board members also were worried about being personally affiliated with an explicitly gay organization: "A lot of people on the board had corporate jobs and things and were just not fully out."[28]

Ultimately, the board's commitment to the clinic's growth and sustainability, rather than to the growth of gay-specific services and organizations linked to gay liberation, drove its decision to focus on gay health services. The board adopted the recommendation to serve the gay and lesbian communities in the summer of 1980.[29] In an effort to avoid tension with existing clients and the larger Fenway neighborhood, the board insisted that services be given to anyone who came to the clinic, regardless of their sexuality, and that the clinic attempt to reach out to gay minorities.[30] Though reluctant at first, the Fenway clinic committed fully to being an organization with a gay and lesbian focus.

For the Fenway clinic, being a gay and lesbian clinic meant redefining gay health. It expanded on the gay health offerings that consisted largely of VD testing to consider gay patients holistically, including their nonsexual health care, mental health needs, and complementary social services. The Fenway clinic and its board proved fully committed to serving gays and lesbians even as their health needs expanded exponentially in the early 1980s. AIDS emerged on the Boston landscape in late 1981, with Fenway Dr. Lenny Alberts diagnosing the first case of the disease in New England.[31] Dr. Kenneth Mayer, a recent transplant from Chicago and veteran Howard Brown Memorial Clinic volunteer, joined the staff and immediately initiated research and community education programs in 1980. He quickly became a researcher and clinician on the forefront of the disease. Within a year of the first Boston AIDS case, the basement Fenway clinic hosted experts from the Centers for Disease Control, the National Institutes of Health, and Harvard Medical School hoping to learn from the clinic's response to the epidemic.[32] The Fenway clinic became a national leader in terms of community-based research, experimental treatments, hospice care, and support groups for patients, community members, and the staff who faced death and trauma to an extent previously unseen in American community health clinics. Prodded further by the needs of the AIDS crisis, the Fenway clinic began defining gay health services as responding to physical, mental, emotional, sexual, and community health needs, rather than as just providing VD testing.

At the same time, the Fenway clinic also expanded its understanding of gay health services to include lesbians. The clinic blazed a trail for lesbians seeking to become mothers through alternative insemination (AI). Though initially hesitant to divert any attention or resources away from the AIDS crisis or draw more critique from the public at a time when AIDS-inspired homophobia peaked, in 1983 the Fenway clinic board approved a proposal, two years in the making, from the Fenway AI Task Force to offer education and insemination services for lesbians wanting to conceive.[33] Among the first in the nation, the AI program at the Fenway clinic became a model for similar services across the country that granted lesbians easier access to fertility services than ever before.[34] While the clinic downplayed its affiliation with the gay and lesbian community in the 1970s, it emerged as a gay and lesbian health gladiator with a newly expanded definition of gay (and lesbian) health after coming out in 1980.

Destigmatizing Sex

Sex positivity proved central to transforming the distrust gay men held for doctors and medicine. The systemic discrimination gay patients experienced in doctors' offices had its foundation in the work of early sexologists, and psychoanalysts later reinforced the stigma and pathological understanding of homosexuality. However, neither sexologists nor psychoanalysts delved significantly into the actual sexual practices of homosexuals, beyond a blanket label of perversity. Doctors understood homosexuality as a sickness without really understanding what constituted homosexual sexual behavior. Most doctors in the 1970s did not know to check the anus or mouth of patients who identified themselves as men having sex with men for VD-related sores, and many medical professionals in the 1980s were slow to encourage gay men to use condoms to avoid HIV transmission.

Gay health clinics, on the other hand, used their often personal knowledge of gay sexual practices to provide useful medical advice as well as to build trust with gay patients. Not surprisingly, within the framework of oppression sickness and with its strong ties to gay liberation, the Los Angeles Gay Community Services Center made great efforts to show its patrons that it not only understood what gay sex could entail but that it was neither squeamish nor embarrassed by it. On the contrary, the center embraced the gay liberation notion of gay love as politically powerful and beautiful, with gay sex serving as the enactment of that beauty and political power. This celebration of and frankness about gay sex permeated the center, appearing in posters, programming, and outreach efforts. Publicity for the VD clinic regularly used sexual innuendo and humor to market clinic services and provide reminders to patients to get tested. Various iterations of posters featuring two naked men embracing with the reminder "Don't give him anything but love" or "Gay love needs care" adorned the center's walls.[35]

These posters also communicated, though more indirectly, that gay sex was not shameful or a sign of sickness, but good and fun. Having a medical care provider, even a gay one, project that message of sex positivity, was unprecedented for many gay patients and revolutionary to their relationship with health-care providers, if only the health-care providers in this very specific gay clinic setting.

In the VD clinic, patients also found their sexual activity understood, acknowledged, and accepted as never before as intake forms invited patients to check boxes for the sexual acts they performed or practices they engaged in. Furthermore, the options on the forms used language familiar to the patient, rather than the more medicalized vernacular of the clinician; "blow job,"

DON'T GIVE HIM ANYTHING BUT LOVE

V.D. TESTING, TREATMENT, & INFORMATION
FREE, CONFIDENTIAL, NO HASSLE, BY GAY BROTHERS...FOR GAY BROTHERS
**men's clinic hours: monday, wednesday, friday, 6 p.m.-9:30 p.m.
saturday, 9 a.m.-12:30 p.m.** (GET HERE DURING THE FIRST HOUR OF CLINIC OPERATION... IT GUARANTEES BEING SEEN!)
THE GAY COMMUNITY SERVICES CENTER
1614 WILSHIRE BOULEVARD, LOS ANGELES, CALIFORNIA, 90017   PHONE (213) 482-3062
GAY PEOPLE WORKING TOGETHER TO SERVE THE NEEDS OF OUR COMMUNITY! JOIN WITH US.

Figure 10. Poster for VD testing at the Los Angeles Gay Community Services Center. "Don't Give Him Anything But Love," box 13, folder 11, L.A. Gay & Lesbian Center Records, Coll2007-010, ONE National Gay & Lesbian Archives, USC Libraries, University of Southern California.

"fisting," and "fucking" became commonly used not only on intake forms at the Los Angeles Gay Community Services Center but on many forms and surveys at gay clinics throughout the country.[36] Before even meeting with a doctor or nurse, patients knew that the clinicians had a vocabulary, acceptance, and expertise in gay sex that rarely existed outside of gay health clinics.

Figure 11. Poster for VD testing at the Los Angeles Gay Community Services Center. "Gay Love Needs Care," box 13, folder 11, L.A. Gay & Lesbian Center Records, Coll2007-010, ONE National Gay & Lesbian Archives, USC Libraries, University of Southern California.

The message was clear: gay patients could trust the clinicians at gay health centers. This, of course, stood in stark contrast to the common and often traumatizing experiences at mainstream doctors' offices or public health clinics, where most gay men remained closeted or encountered ostracism, ignorance, or pathology when they came out.

The center also understood itself not just as a site of gay services or a gay community building, but also as a potential location for social interactions that might lead to sex. Certainly, there were rules and expectations about not actually having sex within the center, though the complaints of some suggest that these rules may have been broken upon occasion.[37] However, the center used its programming to continue to present itself as accepting, even celebratory, of gay sex by hosting regular social events, including dances and evening gatherings, that served to fight oppression sickness by removing the stigma from gay social and sexual interactions.[38] Holding these sorts of events on site was unique to the Los Angeles Gay Community Services Center, as other gay health clinics at the time resided within strict clinical settings. Nonetheless, the approach of destigmatizing gay sex as a means to building trust with gay clients proved an effective strategy, not surprisingly, among gay health clinics and service providers. Furthermore, gay patients were incredibly receptive, as evidenced by the growing patient numbers and success of these clinics. Though far from winning universal trust from all gay patients for all medical care providers, the sex positive strategy among gay health clinics like the Los Angeles Gay Community Services Center created at least some spaces in which gay patients and doctors saw themselves without fear or stigma. In this way, these clinics provided the initial staging ground for recasting the relationship between these two groups on a larger scale while addressing the real medical needs of gay patients. Just as clinicians and researchers recognized gay patient distrust of medical providers as an impediment to the population's health, they also knew that educating mainstream medical providers about gay sex and gay medical needs was a crucial, if difficult, hurdle to clear as well.

Becoming Established: Collaboration, Research, and Vaccines

Gaining the trust of gay patients and expanding clinical understandings of gay health within gay clinics created an unprecedented opportunity to design and conduct medical research that challenged medical understandings of gay health more broadly. By the end of the 1970s, most of the larger and more established gay health clinics across the country, including those in Los Angeles, Boston, and Chicago, had either initiated or made significant plans to create research programs.

Not surprisingly, given its medical origins, the Howard Brown Memorial Clinic in Chicago was a trailblazer in designing, conducting, and publishing gay health–related research. The Howard Brown clinic offered quality, accepting, and free medical care to Chicago's gay community, which in return provided two essential ingredients for conducting medical research: money and data. While money kept the clinic open and eventually allowed it to expand its research capabilities, the support of the community in the form of data was of even greater importance. The clinic's large patient base, combined with the concentration of venereal diseases among the patients, offered a treasure trove for potential research on sexually transmitted diseases, hepatitis (which at the time was only hypothesized to be sexually transmissible), liver function, and intestinal parasites, to name just a few subjects of interest.

In 1976, when the Howard Brown clinic broke away from Gay Horizons and began to pursue medical research in earnest, its greatest research limitations were space and funding. Ostrow, who led the clinic's research efforts throughout the decade, was not able to conduct his own testing because of a lack of physical space and equipment. However, he contributed to the growing medical literature about homosexuality by focusing on topics that did not require him to conduct his own testing. He wrote and coauthored articles on doctor-patient interaction and basic examination practices, which highlighted the idiosyncrasies of gay health and how slight changes in intake questions, examinations, and contact tracing resulted in better quality of care for gay patients.[39] He also drew conclusions through quantitative analyses of clinic patients' testing results provided by city-run testing facilities. While creating research articles without the ability to conduct his own laboratory tests was not sustainable, Ostrow made significant inroads into better educating mainstream medicine and expanding its definition of gay health to include both healthy gay patients and sick gay patients in need of care that accounted for, rather than pathologized, their sexuality. He also compiled enough evidence by tracking trends in the testing results to initiate working relationships with local doctors, agencies, and businesses whose own research interests coincided with the clinic's client samples.

This collaborative approach to research allowed the Howard Brown clinic to challenge outdated and unhelpful understandings of gay health in many ways. First, the clinic fostered the creation and dissemination of research related to gay health in mainstream medicine, which led to more knowledgeable medical professionals, better treatment for gay men in health settings, and improved diagnosis and prevention of disease in gay patients. The local gay newspaper summed up the clinic's intent thus: "The name of the game at Howard Brown is disease control—specifically, those diseases which are transmitted through sexual contact."[40] Second, by inviting a variety of researchers to use the clinic's test results and samples, numerous research projects occurred simultaneously, and published articles became fairly commonplace in medical literature.[41] While Howard Brown doctors actually wrote only a handful of these articles and studies, the clinic in many ways served as a national clearinghouse for gay medical research through its partnerships and growing expertise. As the reputation of the clinic grew, so did the perceived validity of its research among skeptical clinicians. Ostrow and other Howard Brown volunteers corresponded with many of those conducting research on gay health during this period, providing feedback, offering collaboration, or exchanging recent findings.[42] He and other former members of the gay medical students group served as the basis for what evolved into a national network of gay doctors, many with research interests in gay health. Through these collaborative research studies and writings, the content of medical literature regarding homosexuals changed dramatically during the mid-1970s. In the wake of the late 1960s sexual revolution and the more outspoken and militant gay political activism of the early 1970s, discussion of homosexuality all but disappeared from medical literature in the early 1970s, with the exception of news related to the removal of homosexuality from the Diagnostic and Statistical Manual in 1973.[43] Through a wide range of medical journals, in numerous conference proceedings, and even in book-length studies in the second half of the decade, a handful of gay doctors, medical professionals, and academics began to answer questions surrounding gay health, defining it in new ways and disentangling homosexuality from pathology.[44]

The clinic's ability to conduct its own testing and research improved significantly in the fall of 1978, when it moved into a new 4,000-square-foot space in the heart of the emerging gay enclave on North Halsted Street that included 500 square feet of research offices and labs equipped for the processing of all standard sexually transmitted disease tests.[45] While making full use of its new capacities, the clinic also continued collaborating with as many outside researchers and agencies as possible. By teaming with Mason-Barron Laboratories, a private company located in a Chicago suburb that specialized in liver-related testing and research, the Howard Brown clinic was able to provide needed tests and related treatments for its patients with advanced liver damage due to various venereal diseases without having to bear the cost of the expensive laboratory equipment.[46] Despite early disagreements over case tracking and notification protocol, the Howard Brown Memorial Clinic and the Chicago Department of Health went on to enjoy a productive relationship wherein the clinic identified and treated venereal diseases in a previously difficult and elusive community while the city provided advanced laboratory tests, grants, and other logistical supports.[47] By outsourcing its most expensive and specialized tests and collaborating with a wide range of medical professionals and businesses, the Howard Brown Memorial Clinic provided comprehensive care to its patients while building relationships with and redefining gay health for the larger medical community. Consequently, as gay medical research began to flourish in the second half of the 1970s, the Howard Brown Memorial Clinic was at the forefront, often spearheading studies and forging new relationships with funding agencies and pharmaceutical companies.[48]

In each of these new venues, the Howard Brown clinic helped to redefine gay health. While the partnerships and projects recast gay health in new ways and expanded the web of sympathetic professionals linked to the clinic, no project proved more valuable and constructive than the hepatitis B study. In an interview Ostrow recalled, "Very early on, I noticed [while] reviewing all the [test results] that a very high proportion of the men either were recovering from acute hepatitis or came in with symptoms of active hepatitis. . . . It was kind of known in the community . . . that it was an occupational hazard of being gay. But this had never been reported in the literature, it was just folk-lore."[49] A handful of researchers in Australia and England had already noticed the relatively high incidence of hepatitis B in homosexual men and were hypothesizing about it being sexually transmitted, but most in the medical field, certainly those in the United States, believed it could only be "transmitted through dirty needles, through blood donations, contact with blood. It was an occupational exposure for health care workers."[50] In June 1976, Ostrow wrote to a colleague he knew from his time as a student at the University of Chicago, proposing a joint research effort on hepatitis B transmission and prevalence among gay men.[51] Over the next several years, this collaboration grew to include the Howard Brown Memorial Clinic, the University of Chicago, the Chicago Board of Health, the Centers for Disease Control, a handful of other gay clinics across the country, and the pharmaceutical company Merck as the study evolved into the development of a hepatitis B vaccine.

Within months, Ostrow and a handful of doctors at the University of Chicago had developed a comprehensive study to determine if and how hepatitis B transmission could occur sexually. In an effort to provide a broad and diverse sample for study, the research included patients from the Howard Brown Memorial Clinic as well as from "a large public clinic patronized by many homosexual men" in San Francisco.[52] The project required patients who tested positive for hepatitis B to complete an extensive questionnaire about their sexual histories and practices. After many rounds of perfecting the questionnaire, recruiting patients, and gaining the support of all the necessary people at individual clinics and in city health departments, responses were compiled, analyzed, and presented in a journal article published in 1978, after nearly two years of work.[53] The findings proved that hepatitis B could in fact be sexually transmitted and that sexual practices common among gay men were highly effective in transmitting the disease, making gay men a population ripe for further study of the disease, its treatment, and prevention. The lead researchers in the hepatitis B project had long sought involvement from the Centers for Disease Control (CDC) in the hopes of expanding their research to include treatment and prevention for gay patients. As a Howard Brown Memorial Clinic staff update proclaimed in January 1978 after the release of the study's findings, "Our Medical Director [Ostrow] started these conversations with CDC officials two years ago and finally we are seeing the CDC taking an active role in the health needs of the gay male."[54] Ostrow summarized the situation: "The CDC came to me and said . . . Merck [pharmaceutical company] is developing a vaccine, and they are doing their trials on hospital workers [also a high risk group for hepatitis B], but we would love to see if the vaccine works in gay men because if it does then it will be the first vaccine against a sexually transmitted disease."[55] The hepatitis B research expanded the reach and impact of gay health research, redefining not just gay health, but recasting its value and relationship to public health more broadly.

With the involvement of the CDC and Merck, the cast of characters involved in the hepatitis project grew exponentially, reinforcing existing working relationships and creating many new ones.[56] In order to find enough participants for the vaccine trials, the CDC included five clinics, each with a significant gay clientele, in the study: the Howard Brown Memorial Clinic in Chicago, the Los Angeles Gay Community Services Center, and clinics in Denver, San Francisco, and St. Louis. While the project did not require interaction between researchers at individual clinics, as the CDC acted as the project manager, many of the doctors and researchers already knew one another from previous research studies and regularly corresponded.[57] The hepatitis study simply reinforced those relationships and allowed for greater professional networking among many of the doctors concerned with gay health at the time. Together they conducted research that demanded a recalibration of mainstream medicine's understanding of gay health by examining the actual diseases gay patients experienced. With the CDC as the principal manager of the entire study, the Howard Brown clinic gained access to CDC testing facilities and funding, but most importantly, built strong working relationships with many in the contagious and venereal disease divisions of the agency.

Beyond strengthening relationships between medical professionals working on gay health and redefining gay health for mainstream medicine, the hepatitis B study also reinforced new understandings of gay health among gay patients that included trust of clinicians. The Howard Brown clinic solicited participants in a medical trial, asking gay patients to contribute actively rather than simply analyzing test results and questionnaires. Flyers and pamphlets distributed in clinics and in gay businesses, bars, and bathhouses appealed to potential trial participants as people wanting to contribute to the larger society on behalf of "the gay community." One leaflet, after explaining the effect of hepatitis B on gay communities and populations "in the third world" stated, "If the U.S. can make available thru the World Health Organization an effective Hepatitis vaccine we can help prevent thousands of deaths from liver cancer. Gay people will have played an important role in that effort."[58] However, some calls for study participants focused more on the local community and the individual participants. One call for participants explained, "You may help other people in the community be protected against Hepatitis B while at the same time benefiting yourself financially."[59] A call for trial participants appeared in most gay media outlets in the city, but these promotions also sought to dispel any anxiety among gay patients about being used in what amounted to a very well-organized and well-funded medical experiment.[60] In almost every form of publicity that the trial organizers produced, potential participants were reminded that the "vaccine has been safely tested and the present trial is only to determine its efficacy. No-one is being used as a 'guinea pig.'"[61] While most vaccine trials of the period included an explanation of a trial's purpose, the added reassurance that gay patients were not being treated as "guinea pigs" reflects the tumultuous history of the relationship between the gay and medical communities. It also illustrates the Howard Brown clinic's conscious and constant efforts to build and reinforce trust with gay patients in ways that redefine gay health to include at least some aspects of the medical mainstream. The speed with which the trials filled in Chicago, as well as other participating cities, suggests that efforts on the part of gay health activists to foster trust and redefine gay health in this way had been largely successful. One project coordinator, Norman Altman, remarked that "the response from the community has really been fantastic. People have been very dependable about appointments and anxious to enroll in the program."[62] Like many of its other collaborations, the hepatitis B study allowed the Howard Brown Memorial Clinic to strengthen its reputation and capabilities as both a research facility and a health-care service provider for gay patients, enabling it to play a crucial role in redefining gay health in many communities during the 1970s.

Through the vaccine trials and CDC study, the Howard Brown Memorial Clinic, as well as the other clinics involved, became well versed in another important aspect of the medical establishment with which few had previous experience: drug and vaccine development and testing. In the vaccine trials, all participants received regular testing for hepatitis B as well as a dosage of either the vaccine or a placebo. The CDC laboratories processed all the blood work and also determined which dose, vaccine or placebo, patients would receive. Participating clinics, including the Howard Brown Memorial Clinic, were charged with recruiting and following up with participants, drawing blood and shipping it to the CDC testing facility, and disseminating the proper dose to each participant. By comparing the infection rates over the course of a year of those who received the actual vaccine to those who received the placebo, the trials determined that the vaccine was an effective prophylactic for hepatitis B. The hepatitis B vaccine was groundbreaking in a few ways. First, neither the CDC nor any pharmaceutical company had ever worked so closely with gay community clinics or sought out gay trial participants for a vaccine for the general public. The vaccine itself was also a medical innovation.[63] It was the first vaccine for a sexually transmitted disease.[64] Furthermore, it was the first to be derived from a pioneering new process that used the plasma cells from people recovering from acute hepatitis B as the basis for a vaccine. As such, gay men played a central role in the creation of the vaccine as well as its testing as trial participants, and other gay men with acute hepatitis B donated their plasma to develop the vaccine. Ostrow simplified the process when he explained, "The vaccine was being made from recovering people and acutely affected people."[65] The final vaccine was "a very expensive process involving a total of seven steps which takes about 16 months" and was limited by the "very few people eligible to donate blood for this purpose."[66]

The groundbreaking aspects of the vaccine and trials also resulted in some of the greatest problems both for the vaccine and in maintaining new understandings of gay health among both gay patients and mainstream medicine. After the success of the trials, as the vaccine neared its approval and recommendation by the Food and Drug Administration (FDA) in 1981, gay patients balked at the vaccine's projected cost of $190.[67] Many gay men felt that the high cost was a slap in the face after their participation in research studies that had proven the disease was sexually transmittable and their active role in the subsequent vaccine trials.[68] Responding swiftly to the shaken trust of their patients, the Howard Brown Memorial Clinic and a handful of other gay clinics across the country created a Hepatitis Research Fund that would allow for vaccines to be available at a reduced cost for those in need. The frustration over the vaccine's cost also led the clinic to explore "off the record" options for obtaining the vaccine, including working with another locally headquartered pharmaceutical company, Abbott Laboratories, to recreate the vaccine at a lower cost.[69] However, before a substantial battle materialized over the cost of the Merck-produced hepatitis B vaccine, in 1986 the FDA revoked its approval of the vaccine when Chiron Corporation developed a cheaper and safer vaccine production method using yeast rather than plasma.[70] The innovative production process that used plasma from people with hepatitis B posed a perceived health risk in light of the emergence of AIDS. Ostrow recalled the concern: "Since the HIV virus wasn't discovered for four more years, there was no way of knowing if [HIV] survived the purification process for the anti-hepatitis vaccine."[71] Rather than risk transmitting AIDS to vaccine recipients, Merck shelved the vaccine permanently, Abbott abandoned any interest in replicating the new process, and community frustration over cost became irrelevant. A new hepatitis B vaccine, the first vaccine to make the antigen in yeast, gained FDA approval in 1986.

Despite the failure to market the vaccine, the research and collaboration in its successful production and the larger hepatitis B study were a great success for the Howard Brown Memorial Clinic and represented tremendous strides in redefining gay health in mainstream medicine. The hepatitis B work, as well as other smaller collaborative efforts at the clinic, fostered the growth of a gay medical establishment, complete with clinics, research abilities and laboratories, professional networks, and areas of specialization. Through these experiences, gay health professionals and activists in Chicago gained experience navigating nearly every step of the research process, from building trust among patients to designing research projects and from collaborating with national health agencies to dealing with pharmaceutical companies. Through the various research efforts of the Howard Brown Memorial Clinic, clinic doctors not only built a national reputation as a research institution but also consistently maintained the trust and support of gay patients. Mainstream medical professionals had an unprecedented wealth of research from which to learn about the illnesses and effective treatments for gay men, allowing for a new understanding of gay health to replace previous framings that relied on pathology. Meanwhile, by decade's end gay men in Chicago had access to quality health care and could claim pride and partial responsibility for creating research, protocols, and a vaccine that would help communities at large. In short, through medical research, the Howard Brown clinic successfully bridged the long history of division and distrust that had often pitted mainstream medicine against gay patients by fostering new definitions of gay health among both patients and providers.

*   *   *

While the Merck hepatitis B vaccine did not meet the expectations of those who helped in its creation, the project illustrates the success of a much larger undertaking by gay health activists and medical professionals in the 1970s. Like many other groups who felt persecuted, oppressed, or disempowered by mainstream medicine, gay patients and gay health activists challenged the authority of pathologizing doctors in the 1970s. While some gay health proponents, like those in Boston and Los Angeles, focused more on simply providing quality care to gay patients or fighting mainstream medicine's homophobia through political means, the Howard Brown Memorial Clinic in Chicago started a national trend of employing the methods of mainstream medical research to create a new understanding of gay health. In doing so the clinic created medical research that at first filled the very basic gaps in knowledge of homosexuality and then went on to place homosexuals at the center of the creation of a vaccine that was innovative and had great significance to the medical profession, as hepatitis B was an occupational hazard of medicine. Early articles and publications reveal just how little was known about the health needs of gay men at the time as many explored basic questions such as how to give a thorough medical exam to gay men and at what age gay men had their first homosexual experiences.[72] These findings were presented not only in a variety of forms, but also to an array of audiences. Heterosexual medical professionals could learn about gay health through published scientific studies in the *Journal of the American Medical Association*, while bathhouse regulars might learn about sexual health via an article in the local gay newspaper or *The Advocate Guide to Gay Health*.[73] With gay doctors driving the medical discourse around homosexuality, discussion of actual health issues began to replace pathological assumptions regarding homosexuality on the part of individual medical professionals and distrust of mainstream medicine among gay patients. In this way, the focus on medical research contributed to the successful reframing of the relationship between the gay and medical communities in the 1970s and a widespread redefinition of gay health.

Marshaling numerous resources within the community, ranging from protest to publication of research, gay health activism of the 1970s inaugurated a significant change in the way the gay and medical communities interacted with one another. Gay health activists often rewrote the rules of public health and medical protocol, as in the cases of anonymous testing and exams that included anal and throat cultures for men, to create safer, more effective, and higher-quality health care for gays. As a result, they began to mend the historically bad relationship between the two groups by rebuilding trust and improving care. However, they also went to great lengths to encourage the medical field at large to become more informed and understanding about gay health needs. Certainly, homosexuality and sexuality in general remained controversial in the medical professions beyond the 1970s, but the research and outreach/education efforts championed by gay health activists of the decade made significant and historically unprecedented progress in diminishing and defusing that stigma. Through collaboration, publication, research, and networking, gay health activists challenged mainstream medicine's understanding and approach to gay health, resulting in better lines of communication between the two communities and greater knowledge about disease transmission and treatment in gay populations.

This multifaceted renegotiation of gay health required and spurred communication between gay patients and gay clinics, gay medical professionals and their straight counterparts, and between gay service providers across the country. The sharing of research and best practices instigated meaningful relationships between clinics, marking the next important evolutionary step in gay health activism during the decade. The relationships developed between doctors and researchers in Denver, Los Angeles, New York, and Chicago on the hepatitis B vaccine project proved lasting and extended into other medical issues they saw in their research and patients. Fostering these new partnerships and collaborations, the drive to recast gay health also sparked the creation of a national gay health infrastructure well seasoned with a blend of political origins, savvy about state interactions, and dedicated to serving gay patients. This infrastructure ensured that gay health activism would eventually extend beyond the confines of local clinics and the limits of clinic-specific politics and prove instrumental in the early AIDS crisis of the 1980s.

CHAPTER 5

THE GAY HEALTH NETWORK MEETS AIDS

By the end of the 1970s, gay health activism had transformed from a few shoestring pop-up clinics to a full-fledged gay medical infrastructure that included clinics, outreach programs, research, and ties with mainstream medical professional and research organizations at both the local and the national levels. Understandings of and approaches to gay health had changed dramatically, so that gay patients and medical professionals saw one another as potential partners in health. Clinics proved the lifeblood of this transformation. Thus, the national infrastructure reflected the varied origins of the community clinics on which it relied, implementing research and networking tools to improve health *and* challenge political oppression. The new national networks, too, like their local clinic counterparts, relied on personal relationships that bridged political movements, medical professions, and state borders.

This vibrant, multifaceted, and seasoned gay health infrastructure of the 1970s became the network of first responders in the early AIDS crisis. Between 1981, when the first reports of rare forms of both pneumonia and cancer among gay men marked the start of the epidemic, and 1985, when the FDA licensed the first commercial HIV test, gay health clinics played a vital role in shaping the initial response to the epidemic. Whether stand-alone clinics, mobile vans, or outposts within gay bathhouses, these facilities were frequently the first in their city or region to come into contact with AIDS and remained on the frontline of the crisis throughout the decade.[1]

As a direct result of the work of the previous decade, the clinics and their related gay health networks were well equipped for the AIDS epidemic. They had the trust of gay patients. Clinic practitioners and researchers had robust professional networks through which they could share information quickly. Many of the major clinics had already established research programs and had cultivated well-informed and gay-friendly working relationships with officials at the CDC. Perhaps most importantly, every aspect of the gay medical landscape had been built to address patient needs that were poorly understood, highly stigmatized, and garnered little interest or funding from mainstream medicine and policy. While the early AIDS crisis proved unprecedented in scale, mortality, and stigma, it also illuminated some of the greatest strengths of the gay medical networks developed in the 1970s.

Building a National Network

While each clinic emerged from its own particular political milieu and evolved in distinctive ways over the decade, as a group, clinics played an important role in the emergence of a national network, serving as a foundation for the burgeoning gay health structure. Most importantly clinics provided physical spaces in which patients, volunteers, and practitioners intermingled in meaningful ways. In clinics, these groups discussed health, naming and dissecting political and medical needs and hurdles. They conceptualized and conducted research. As such, clinics served as a gateway through which patients became activists, practitioners sought out others facing the same challenges, and perspectives of gay health shifted. As practitioners and volunteers began building both formal and informal networks to exchange ideas, share research, and organize politically and professionally, clinics remained a central and grounding entry point that supplied doctors, volunteers, patients, and research data. National gay health organizations and networks emanated from the needs of patients, volunteers, or practitioners in the clinical setting. The needs of patients and their care providers inspired dozens of both formal and informal national groups and directly informed political, professional, and research agendas. This interdependence linking the clinics, and specifically, patients and practitioners therein, with the national networks and organizations that emerged over the 1970s became a hallmark and great strength of the resulting gay medical infrastructure by decade's end.

By the end of the 1970s, the clinics in Boston, Los Angeles, and Chicago represented just a small part of a nationwide gay medical network. More than two dozen gay community clinics existed across the country, from the Atlanta Gay Center to the Seattle Clinic for Venereal Health and from the Metro Detroit Gay VD Council to the Montrose Clinic in Houston.[2] Most of these clinics, like the Los Angeles Gay Community Services Center and the Fenway Community Health Clinic, offered only limited hours of operation and on-site testing for venereal diseases.[3] Yet, even with their limited capacities, these clinics, like those in Boston, Chicago, and Los Angeles, often had reputations among health departments and clinicians as "umpteen times better than any other public or private facility in town."[4] In addition to clinic-based testing, a growing number of clinics had greater service offerings. Between the three gay health organizations operating in New York City at the dawn of the 1980s (Gay Men's Health Project, St. Mark's Health Center, and Robert Livingston Health Center), gay New Yorkers had easy access to VD testing, treatment, and education in clinic settings, through VD van programs, and even in testing facilities within the city's largest bathhouses.[5] Health activists working at the Whitman-Walker Gay Men's VD Clinic in Washington, D.C., and the Gay Community Center of Baltimore VD Clinic had incorporated a mobile VD testing program, like the one started in Chicago and emulated in Los Angeles in 1975 and Boston in 1978, into their offerings by the end of the 1970s.[6] Gay community clinics in New York and the Whitman-Walker clinic in Washington also became important participants in gay medical research in the late 1970s, often teaming with area public health officials and researchers on studies and publications.[7]

In addition to services originating in gay clinics, the gay medical landscape at the start of the 1980s also consisted of a number of city-run health clinics and outreach programs, illustrating the progress made in challenging institutional homophobia within mainstream medicine. In St. Louis, Denver, and San Francisco, city-run health clinics with a predominantly gay clientele not only offered gay-friendly testing services and mobile VD van programs, but also participated in research, including the hepatitis B study, with other gay community clinics and the CDC.[8] In addition to these clinics and mobile testing programs, gay health activism also materialized in permanent testing facilities within a number of major bathhouses across the country, including New York City's St. Mark's Baths, Chicago's Man's Country, and North Hollywood's Corral Club Baths.[9]

This expansive network of gay health activists, clinics, and organizations also infused gay sexual and political culture with a knowledge and concern for sexual health in the period before AIDS. One newspaper's "Guide to Gay Life" in Chicago proclaimed in 1975 that by "recognizing the problem of venereal disease and the special sensitivities of gay people about getting checked for it . . . health has also become a major concern of gay activities."[10] By recruiting help from gay businesses, newspapers, and entertainers, health activists educated gay men about disease symptoms, testing, and treatment while also mending the relationship between gays and medicine. This widespread concern for sexual health within the gay community challenges the typical portrayal of gay sexual culture in the era before AIDS particularly as it relates to health. The 1970s saw the greatest concern for gay sexual health of any prior period, and gay health activists of the time proved highly effective in creating a gay medical framework. Simply put, gay health mattered in the 1970s, and gay health activism and services not only existed but flourished in the decade.

Clinical services were just one part of the gay health infrastructure built in the 1970s. A network of gay medical professionals also emerged during this period that connected people from all over the country and from numerous areas of medical specialization. Illuminating both the centrality of personal relationships to the emergence of a national gay health infrastructure and its close ties to political activism, many of the gay medical professional organizations of the 1970s can be traced back to the living room of one Philadelphia public health professional. Walter Lear initiated the development of a gay professional network that grew to include nearly two dozen gay professional organizations by the end of the decade. Lear was commissioner of health services for the Southeastern Region of the Pennsylvania Departments of Health and Public Welfare in 1975 and a longtime health activist. He had been a founding member of the Medical Committee for Human Rights in 1964, a group of American physicians that provided health care to civil rights activists during the Freedom Rides. He was also a longtime proponent of social medicine and dear friend to Chicago-based social medicine authority Quentin Young (who had strongly influenced David Ostrow's political understanding of health care during his undergraduate years at the University of Chicago).[11] In 1975, the fifty-one-year-old Lear had also just come out publicly as a gay man.[12] Free from the closet in which he had lived for over twenty years, Lear explained that "coming out for me also meant both a political act and a service commitment."[13] Within weeks of coming out, Lear set his sights on creating a caucus of gay public health workers within the American Public Health Association (APHA) and getting the association to pass a comprehensive gay rights resolution at its 1975 annual meeting in Chicago. The purpose of the gay rights resolution was to raise awareness and get formal support from the APHA for gay rights both within the organization and in the giving of care to gay and lesbian patients by association members. Describing his early attempts at building the caucus, Lear remembered, "First of all, I approached the public health workers I knew to be gay; all were closeted as there were no openly gay APHA members. These requests for help in getting the Caucus started were rejected—several even tried to persuade me to drop the project. So I recruited health workers through personal contacts in gay political circles and ads in the gay press."[14] Despite early recruiting setbacks, the gay caucus that arrived in Chicago in November for the APHA's annual meeting consisted of roughly twenty members from all across the country. Lesbians constituted a third of the caucus, demonstrating how national networks often proved more welcoming

Figure 12. Volunteers staff the first gay caucus booth at the American Public Health Association's annual meeting in 1975. Photograph taken by Walter Lear and gifted to author as part of oral interview. Walter Lear, interview by author, May, 21, 2007.

Figure 13. Gay caucus members chatting in a hotel room at the American Public Health Association's annual meeting in 1975. Photograph taken by Walter Lear and gifted to author as part of oral interview. Walter Lear, interview by author, May, 21, 2007.

and productive for lesbians than the often sexist and politically rife local clinic settings. Equipped with printed brochures, an inviting booth, and even a hospitality suite, the caucus members lobbied hard during the three-day meeting until, on the final day, the APHA Governing Council adopted the entire gay rights resolution proposed by the gay caucus.[15] The APHA was the first large and mainstream professional medical organization to acknowledge and support its gay membership. With this major victory, the gay caucus of the APHA returned to Lear's living room in Philadelphia to continue its fight against institutional homophobia in the medical profession.

The sun-filled living room in Lear's large Victorian house transformed into a war room of sorts, as it hosted the diverse membership of the caucus, which included medical professionals and amateur health activists from all across the country. In their battle to correct the failures of mainstream medicine in dealing with gay patients' medical needs, Lear's living room became a place of refuge, collaboration, and political plotting. Members of the caucus shared questions, research, funding ideas, failures, and success stories. The appearance of mobile or bathhouse-based VD testing programs in a number of cities, including Denver, Baltimore, Minneapolis, and Pittsburgh, resulted in part from conversations and relationships built in that room.[16] Participants, including regular attendees David Ostrow from Chicago and Ron Vachon from Fenway, brainstormed about how to build trust between the gay and medical communities, and ultimately to provide better care for gay patients. The official business of the caucus meetings focused more on improving the standing of gay and lesbian medical professionals within the larger medical profession.[17] However, the conversations and collaborations that took place before and after meetings, between agenda items, and in letters and phone calls between caucus members engaged gay health in a very hands-on, street-level way. The caucus provided a venue for gay health professionals and activists to communicate, strategize, and network. Consequently, Lear's living room became a clearinghouse for the majority of gay health clinics, outreach

Figure 14. Walter Lear's home. His living room, on the left on the first floor, proved a critical site of collaboration for many gay health activist efforts across the country, particularly organizing gays and lesbians within national medical professional associations. Photograph courtesy of Monica Mercado.

programs, and other forms of gay health activism in the second half of the 1970s.[18]

The activism of the gay caucus of the APHA was quickly replicated in other medical professional associations in the late 1970s, often under the direction of APHA gay caucus members who held memberships in multiple medical professional organizations. The result was a vast and diverse network of gay medical professionals and organizations that were in close contact with one another. By 1978, gay caucuses also appeared within the professional organizations for guidance counselors, sex educators, therapists, medical students, nurses, and substance abuse workers as well as in the American Psychological Association, the American Psychiatric Association, and the National Association of Social Workers.[19] Even the historically conservative American Medical Association had a caucus of gay and lesbian members by the end of the decade.[20] As a result, discussions of gay health concerns expanded far beyond Lear's Philadelphia house and small gay community clinics. By the start of the 1980s, the annual meetings of many medical professional organizations included research presentations on gay health issues and proved important sites for battling institutional homophobia and building a stronger gay health framework.

The development and testing of the hepatitis B vaccine also played an instrumental role in building a strong gay national health infrastructure in the late 1970s. Clinics in San Francisco, Chicago, Denver, New York, and other cities included in the clinical trials for the Merck vaccine increased communication with one another as they navigated relationships with the CDC, and, later, brainstormed ways to make the costly vaccine more affordable for their patients.[21] Beyond this relatively small circle of correspondents, the hepatitis B vaccine program brought a much larger swath of gay health practitioners together in two ways. First, Merck's manufacturing of the vaccine required the plasma of people either with or recovering from acute hepatitis B. By partnering with gay health clinics across the country, including but not limited to those that went on to participate in the vaccine trials, the CDC and Merck gained access to fairly large populations eligible to donate plasma. At one point in 1983, before it shelved the vaccine in light of the AIDS crisis, the pharmaceutical company contracted with David Ostrow to identify and correspond with all the gay health clinics in the country from which it could solicit plasma and market the vaccine once available.[22] The resulting correspondence among clinicians across the country reinforced strong working relationships.

The hepatitis B vaccine also added fuel to the emergence of specifically gay health conferences and networks in the late 1970s. Regional, national, and increasingly specialized lesbian and gay health conferences became common practice in the second half of the decade. By June 1978, activists and practitioners gathered for the first annual national lesbian and gay health conference. As the national conference grew each year, the panel offerings expanded in number and breadth, spanning a full spectrum of topics, ranging from gay and lesbian mental health needs to clinician burn-out, and from sex education in schools to deaf gay community building, by 1980.[23] Within these larger conferences, clinicians, activists, and researchers particularly focused on sexually transmitted diseases and the hepatitis B vaccine strengthened their networks, creating miniconferences within larger meetings and eventually, creating their own conferences. The first conference specifically on gay STDs, the Current Aspects of Sexually Transmitted Diseases Symposium held in Chicago in June 1979, showcased the work of many gay health researchers across the country, including those involved with the hepatitis B vaccine. The vaccine also provided new avenues by which gay health clinicians and researchers could educate mainstream medicine and improve the quality of care for gay patients beyond gay health clinics, as they presented on the vaccine at mainstream medical conferences, including the International Symposium on Viral Hepatitis in New York City in April 1981.[24]

Beyond caucusing within existing professional medical associations and establishing a regular battery of conferences to foster gay health networks, gay medical professionals of the late 1970s also created new organizations to encourage better communication and increased collaboration between those working on specific gay health issues. One of the most important of these new organizations, the National Coalition of Gay STD Services, actually formed at the Chicago Current Aspects of Sexually Transmitted Diseases Symposium in June 1979. Chaired by Mark Behar, a gay health worker in Milwaukee, the National Coalition of Gay STD Services consisted of gay VD service providers. The narrow and directed focus of the group proved its greatest strength, as it continued to operate for more than a decade. The purpose of the coalition was "to establish a communication network between the nation's gay STD services for sharing ideas about research, fundraising, patient and staff education, procedures and protocols, public relations, etc. [Also] to establish an ongoing liaison between representatives of the Centers for Disease Control and all members of the Coalition."[25] In short, the National Coalition of Gay STD Services' newsletters, meetings, and conferences created formal venues for information exchanges between gay STD service providers, as well as a clear communication channel between the gay community and the CDC. Starting in 1980, the newsletter included a regular back-and-forth discussion between coalition members and Dr. Paul Wiesner, director of the VD Control Division at the CDC, regarding various gay sexual health issues, including access to the then forthcoming hepatitis B vaccine. These dialogues transformed into professional relationships when Wiesner presented the keynote address at a conference sponsored by the coalition in 1980.[26]

The open exchange with Wiesner illustrates the meaningful relationships and spirit of collaboration the new gay medical networks fostered with "straight" institutions, including numerous research universities and state-sponsored entities, such as the CDC. The existence of these productive relationships stands in stark contrast to the confrontation that epitomized the relationship between mainstream medicine and gay health in previous decades. By the end of the 1970s, many of the leading gay health researchers held affiliations with an array of medical schools, served as assistants to local health departments, and garnered international recognition for their research, particularly around hepatitis B.[27] Not only were gay health activists and researchers making tremendous strides in their research, but mainstream institutions increasingly welcomed and valued their input. In 1980, the CDC announced in the National Coalition of Gay STD Services newsletter that its VD Control Division would sponsor a working meeting in Atlanta the summer of the following year designed to "establish a gay STD research priority list to aid . . . in the allocation of [federal] research monies," and ensure continued collaboration between gay health clinics and the CDC.[28]

Even as mainstream medical institutions sought out greater information and collaboration with gay health clinics and researchers, gay patients remained the bedrock of the new gay medical infrastructure. Consequently, as the gay medical networks and research grew in size and scope, so too did the outreach to gay communities and patients. The National Coalition of Gay STD Services collaborated with numerous other national gay health organizations to create, update, and circulate "Guidelines and Recommendations for

Healthful Gay Sexual Activity," a multipage pamphlet sent to public health departments across the country and reprinted in numerous gay newspapers. Though other publications, including books, began to appear with increasing regularity in the late 1970s, "Guidelines" was the most widespread publication and offered the best overview. These guidelines, and their evolution over the final years of the 1970s and into the 1980s, provide a snapshot, in layperson language, of the various diseases afflicting gay patients as well as the most cutting-edge recommendations for "healthful" sexual activity. With matter-of-fact references to "rimming," "getting fucked," and "cock sucking," the guidelines demonstrated a broad knowledge and comfort with various gay sexual practices that made the pamphlet appealing and relevant to gay patients and communities. Predating the concept of "safe sex" and the first hints of the coming AIDS crisis, the suggested safety precautions centered on hygiene and regular testing for VD. However, the 1981 version did recommend that "the use of condoms (rubbers) for anal intercourse will protect against the spread of syphilis and gonorrhea and may even offer protection against herpes, hepatitis B, nongonococcal urethritis and proctitis (these latter four claims are not proven). High quality condoms should be used since breakage may occur more frequently with anal intercourse than with vaginal intercourse." It was among the first to recommend condoms for gay men.[29] The spread of this and similar publications that educated patients and community members about gay sexual health was a linchpin in the emergence of a gay medical infrastructure.

Shifting Landscape

The year 1981 proved a turning point for gay health in many ways, even setting aside the emergence of AIDS. The swearing in of President Ronald Reagan in January 1981 solidified, at a national level, the encroaching fiscal and social conservatism that gay health clinics and service providers had been navigating at the local level during the final years of the 1970s. Gay health clinics, researchers, and activists felt the effects of the new administration almost immediately. While campaigning for president, Reagan had proposed a new fiscal policy for the country that offered significant tax cuts to individuals and corporations and reallocated domestic appropriations to bolster the national defense budget. Throughout the campaign, many public health and gay health activists spoke out against the costs of slashing domestic budgets, particularly those for health and human services. As President Reagan and congressional Republicans began to craft a budget after his inauguration, activists began to protest. On June 2, 1981, Walter Lear and eleven other prominent doctors, public health workers, and health activists breached the White House grounds, kneeling in prayer before being arrested for unlawful entry. The action kicked off a month of "prayer and resistance" organized by a mix of health and pacifist groups "to resist the sacrifice of the poor on the altar of military spending."[30] Yet the introduction of the budget bill just two weeks later on June 19, 1981, showed the full extent to which their concerns had fallen upon deaf ears. Gaining the president's signature on August 13, 1981, the legislation delivered on Reagan's campaign promises, and funding for health services fell in painful ways for gay health clinics and researchers.[31]

Gay health advocates continued to wage battle against the new administration's changes to health care, with Lear testifying against the confirmation of surgeon general nominee C. Everett Koop. In the eyes of Lear and many other gay health advocates, Koop's statements that both the "Gay Pride Movement" and the feminist movement were "anti-family" posed a threat to gay health and gay health programs.[32] Congress confirmed Koop in November, ignoring the pleas of gay clinicians and advocates. Their political and budgetary losses only worsened. The state, it appeared, was transforming from the antiqueer state of the 1970s back toward the "straight state" of the earlier decades of the twentieth century, which had perpetrated structural violence against sexual minorities by cutting off funding, stigmatizing their identities and practices, and willfully ignoring and/or stymieing their needs in policy.[33]

The long-cultivated relationships with supportive individuals at the CDC could not shield gay health from the funding realities imposed by the Reagan budget and the surgeon general's priorities. The July 1981 newsletter for the National Coalition of Gay STD Services announced, with a sobering headline, "CDC Sponsored Gay STD Research Priorities Meeting Postposed Indefinitely." The related article reflected the frustration, uncertainty, and hope for aid from CDC friends that coalition members had in the immediate aftermath of Reagan's first budget; it reported that "the Reagan Administration's slashing of human service needs from the Federal budget. . . . will redefine the CDC's and the VD Control Division's programming priorities. . . . however longtime friend of gay VD programs Dr. Paul Wiesner, [CDC] VD Control Division Director, stated he didn't think gay VD services will be ignored."[34] The will for and interest in continued collaboration existed on both sides, but the funding and direction from the state quickly faded. Gay health advocates braced themselves for the "disastrous" replacement of direct federal funding of programs and projects, which had been an important part of the creation and growth of gay research programs in the face of cash-strapped, inefficient, and homophobic state public health departments, with block grants to individual states for public health services.[35] Gay health activists knew that such an approach would starve many gay-focused research projects and force the closing of many gay clinics without a significant influx of cash from other funding sources or the community. Meanwhile, friends in the CDC waited to see how the budget cuts changed their focus and directed their research partnerships. In 1981, both CDC insiders and clinicians on the ground waited nervously to see just how bad their financial reality had become.

Amid the budget cuts, increased political rancor, precarious research programs, and belt tightening for local gay community clinics, patients threw yet another complicating factor into the shifting gay health landscape. In the last few years of the 1970s, patients appeared to be suffering from seemingly more stubborn and resistant strains of the same venereal diseases common in the gay community. Clinicians took note, sharing information, hoping that the upcoming availability of the hepatitis B vaccine would allow them to focus their efforts on new research and new prevention methods for other venereal diseases. The May 22, 1981, *Morbidity & Mortality Weekly Reports* (*MMWR*), the official weekly publication of the CDC and U.S. Department of Health and Human Services that tracked new disease occurrences, brought attention to an outbreak of spectinomycin-resistant penicillinase-producing Neisseria gonorrhoeae, a new strain of drug-resistant gonorrhea, among gay men.[36] The same publication, just two weeks later, tracked the appearance of Pneumocystis pneumonia, a strain of pneumonia usually seen only in people with severely compromised immune systems, among a small number of previously healthy-seeming gay men. In July *MMWR* reported that Kaposi's sarcoma, a form of cancer typically associated with much older Italian or Eastern European Jewish men, had suddenly begun to appear among small groups of gay men in New York and California.[37] That same month, an article by a Los Angeles clinician in the official newsletter of the National Coalition of Gay STD

Services reported, "The Men's Clinic of the Gay and Lesbian Community Services Center in Hollywood, aside from the usual overwhelming load of cases of gonorrhea, syphilis, and NGU/NGP has recently been seeing even more with symptoms of enteric infections such as amebiasis."[38] Though seemingly unrelated, all of these events happened within six weeks of one another, and many clinicians knew immediately that all of them posed "dangerous" and "noteworthy" threats to gay health.[39] In short, clinicians saw many of their patients with greater frequency, coming in sicker, and slower to recover. The AIDS epidemic had begun.

While the first reports of what would become AIDS appeared in 1981, the actual historical events surrounding those reports reveal much more uncertainty, confusion, and ambiguity than simply pinning the epidemic's start date to a timeline. Researchers and clinicians did not experience AIDS as if a monster disease had suddenly appeared. More aptly, AIDS began to take shape in a medical and political atmosphere that was so different and swiftly changing from that of the previous decade that it was as if clinicians had been blindfolded, taken somewhere else, given a weak flashlight to determine their new surroundings without knowing the basic parameters of their new domain, and *then* a monster disease appeared. As outbreaks of new diseases appeared, and common diseases began to respond atypically, gay health activists and clinicians were already responding to a new and unprecedented fiscal and political crisis for gay health. In addition, they were already addressing a newly understood viral medical epidemic in the gay community in new and groundbreaking ways with the hepatitis B vaccine. In 1981, the ground of gay health shifted in so many ways and so quickly that no one yet knew the contours of the new landscape.

Mobilizing Around AIDS

As the disease slowly came into clearer focus, the AIDS crisis in the early 1980s tested and strengthened the gay medical infrastructure built over the 1970s, which now found itself unexpectedly on the frontlines of one of the largest and deadliest epidemics in recent history. Though activists and health professionals built these networks, organizations, and relationships to address the epidemic proportions of VD within gay male communities, the magnitude, mysteriousness, and morbidity of AIDS strained the existing gay health infrastructure, just as it did all health services. However, even without knowing that the AIDS epidemic was coming, the gay medical infrastructure was set up in such a way that it was able to mount a meaningful AIDS response, even in the face of the new political and economic realities.

Many of the first reported AIDS cases across the country came from clinics and clinicians affiliated with the new gay medical landscape. With both the trust of their patients and an increasingly strong research component in many of the larger clinics, gay community health services became ground zero of the emerging response to the epidemic. If gay community health clinics had been bustling places in the 1970s, the epidemic of the 1980s made them frantic as clinics expanded services to address the constantly growing and changing needs of patients with AIDS. Doctors and public health officials struggled to understand the very basics of the new disease: how it spread, whether it was viral or bacterial, how to determine if someone had transmitted it or not. In fact the CDC and AIDS activists contested and constantly shifted definitions of the disease, and how to diagnose it, for more than a decade. They debated, for example, whether patients had to exhibit a certain type or number of opportunistic diseases before being diagnosed with AIDS. Did they have to meet a certain low threshold of T cells or high threshold of viral loads? Did they have to die? Could only men get AIDS? One doctor lamented in 1983, "The list of putative AIDS agents keeps growing almost as fast as the number of cases. . . . each has failed one or more of the tests for single causative agent."[40] Yet, even without this most basic information about what caused the disease and how it operated, patients came to gay community health clinics looking for information and care.

Though the first treatments would not be FDA approved for six years and would not prove widely effective for fifteen years, gay community health clinics played an instrumental role in identifying and developing meaningful and needed services for their patients and care providers from the very start of the epidemic. In October 1981, the Fenway clinic offered two Friday night AIDS information sessions to communicate the little information it knew about the new disease and its best guesses about prevention; both nights had overflow crowds. With quickly mounting needs, the Fenway and other gay community clinics expanded their services to include "Buddy" programs, which provided mental health care for patients, for friends and family members of people with

AIDS, and for the clinicians trained to cure people who suddenly could not be cured. Though not the life-saving treatments that patients and doctors longed for, these palliative care services served an important purpose for patients, communities, and providers in the fast-moving and deadly new reality. One provider remembered of the early 1980s, "When I think of the number of people I knew who have died, it feels every year since AIDS began is a dog year—like each one counts for seven. That's the only way I can describe what it feels like."[41] Throughout much of the 1980s, the Fenway clinic offered three separate support groups just for its volunteers and clinicians facing the grim realities of the epidemic. The Fenway clinic also responded by creating the AIDS Action Committee, directed by board member Larry Kessler, to design and implement the needed programs. In a 1989 interview, Kessler described the tiny makeshift space in the back of the already crammed basement clinic designated for the volunteer hotline and the three staff members who ran the committee's programs: "Fenway gave us part of a storage room that was filled to the ceiling with carpeting and some field tables from World War I."[42] The small space did not limit the AIDS Action Committee: it soon staffed the volunteer hotline, provided education and outreach to community members, offered services for people with AIDS, and trained hospital workers caring for patients with AIDS.

Gay community health clinics were not just the first stop for patients; they also played a pivotal and dynamic role for mainstream medical leaders and organizations trying to better understand the disease. The Howard Brown Memorial Clinic, the Los Angeles Gay Community Services Center, and the Fenway Community Health Clinic all played host to local doctors and researchers from medical schools and hospitals whom they briefed on the latest developments as well as the treatments they thought useful.[43] In 1982, the Fenway clinic hosted a conference with attendees and speakers from the CDC, Harvard, and the community.[44] These meetings and conferences built on relationships initiated in the 1970s. When AIDS emerged, Harold Jaffe, one of Ostrow's big collaborators in the initial hepatitis B study in 1976, had moved on to a position in the Contagious Diseases Division within the CDC. He, along with Paul Wiesner of the VD Control Division, would become a key figure in the immediate CDC response to the early AIDS crisis and a frequent correspondent of many doctors serving gay patients. Ken Mayer, a member of the Ostrow-founded gay medical students group during his medical training at Northwestern in Chicago, moved to Boston in 1978 for his residency and became the driving force behind research at the Fenway clinic as well as one of the doctors consulted when another Fenway doctor identified the first AIDS case in New England.[45] These relationships lay at the heart of the early medical responses to the AIDS crisis, so that when the first national meetings on what would later be called AIDS took shape, veterans of 1970s gay health activism had seats at the tables.[46]

"Studies have shown more than 90 percent of gay men who develop AIDS have 'markers' that indicate they have already had exposure to hepatitis B."

—Dr. Kenneth Mayer, staff physician, Fenway Community Health Center

Figure 15. Dr. Ken Mayer, member of the gay medical students group in Chicago before moving to Boston, where he became the driving force behind the burgeoning Fenway clinic research program. Neil Miller, "The Hard Sell of a New Vaccine," *Boston Phoenix*, January 10, 1984, section 2. Courtesy of the Archives and Special Collections at Northeastern University, Boston.

Beyond these individual relationships, the past collaborations between organizations also proved central to the AIDS response. Gay professional caucuses and the newsletter of the National Coalition of Gay STD Services became important vehicles of communication among various health professionals, organizations, and government agencies as the AIDS epidemic took shape. Following the very first reports of Kaposi's sarcoma and Pneumocystis pneumonia, the newsletter printed, on the front page and above the fold, both the mailing address and direct phone number for Dr. Jim Curran, the chief of the VD Control Division at the CDC.[47] Just as had been the case with hepatitis B, the CDC turned to the networks of gay health activists and medical professionals to aid in their understanding of the disease, how it spread, and how to stop it. The trust cultivated over the course of the 1970s by gay health activists with the gay community also helped mediate early discussions between bathhouse owners and public health officials over how to contain the disease.[48] While public health officials closed the bathhouses in San Francisco in 1984, Chicago bathhouses were remodeling their physical spaces, with the advice of Ostrow and others, so as to be sites of AIDS education and to encourage only sexual acts that did not transmit the virus, through the removal of private spaces and the creation of glory hole rooms.[49] While treatments took many years to develop, in large part because of the slow identification of HIV, the retrovirus responsible for AIDS, the relationships with pharmaceutical companies and the knowledge of drug trials gained though the hepatitis B vaccine would prove useful as AIDS activists fought to speed the drug approval process and demand affordable treatments.

Even the gay medical research of the previous decade played a crucial role in the early AIDS response. As doctors and researchers struggled to understand and define the new disease, Ostrow quickly realized that the hepatitis B vaccine development and trials offered "a huge lead on research to figure out the natural history of AIDS . . . the people who participated in the hepatitis study in the mid- to late-70s, we had their blood samples all stored away at the CDC and we had their sexual behavior all tracked during that time."[50] Upon learning of the new outbreaks of opportunistic infections, Ostrow immediately reached out to local partners at the Northwestern University Medical School, the CDC, and other gay health actors to initiate research discussions on how to use the hepatitis B data to better understand this new disease. They designed a research study that would utilize the data offered by samples collected for the hepatitis B vaccine program and "helped by the willingness of both patients and healthy gay men participating in our hepatitis B vaccine studies to undergo immunological testing."[51] This collaboration resulted in a grant proposal submitted to the National Cancer Institute on October 22, 1982, which won approval but, because of the budget cuts, was not funded. Ostrow had already honed his skills at redeploying testing results and data from one project to understand another health issue; in the 1970s, he had used VD testing results from state labs to prove the sexual transmissibility of hepatitis B. However, such a piecemeal and indirect approach seemed an impossible response to the AIDS epidemic.

Gay health activists and researchers quickly realized that the AIDS crisis of the 1980s would again require framing their health issues as political issues and acting accordingly. In the new budgetary and political landscape, obtaining even the smallest amount of federal research funding required not only sound research but also political wherewithal. Veterans of not only gay health medicine, but also a wide array of 1970s political movements, the people who were at nearly every level of the new national gay medical infrastructure, plotted their political response. Ron Vachon, the former heart of the gay men's health night at the Fenway clinic, had moved in 1980 to New York City and quickly found himself immersed in AIDS health and service organizing there. Like Lear, Vachon began to mount the next gay health political battle alongside Reagan's campaign and ascension to the White House, writing in December 1981, "If you deplore the current diversion of federal funds for health and human services and the concomitant increase in military spending; if you oppose the Reagan Administration's attack on human rights and the erosion of personal rights in this country and abroad . . . contact: Ron Vachon."[52] By September of the following year, the AIDS crisis had sharpened Vachon's focus and passion, so that he asked Mark Behar to share his three-page handout entitled "Gay Non-Profit Organizations *Can* Have Political Clout!" with the National Coalition of Gay STD Services membership to ease fears of losing tax-exempt status. Stung and frustrated by the approval without funding from the National Cancer Institute, Ostrow testified before the House Labor, Health and Human Services, and Education Appropriations Subcommittee at the Capitol on the inadequacy of federal AIDS funding and policies. Shortly after his testimony, Congress appropriated additional funds for AIDS research, including the research Ostrow had proposed to the National Cancer Institute.[53] While these and similar efforts to engage AIDS as a political issue predated ACT UP, the direct action activist group founded in New York in 1987, by many years, and their results were small scale in the face of the epidemic, they initiated research projects that proved incredibly important for understanding AIDS and its long-term effects.

While the victory of funding for Ostrow's natural history of AIDS project, which came to be called the Multicenter AIDS Cohort (MAC) Study, did not represent the opening of the proverbial floodgates of federal AIDS funding, it did demonstrate both the tenacity and long-term research approach that epitomized the gay medical infrastructure's research response to the early AIDS epidemic. With limited federal funding remaining a barrier to research throughout the 1980s, most AIDS research relied on strong working relationships between researchers within the gay medical infrastructure and beyond, linking gay health clinics with laboratories and investigators at Harvard, Northwestern, UCLA, and elsewhere. These collaborations proved fruitful. In 1984, shortly after HIV had been pinpointed as the cause of AIDS, the Fenway clinic became one of the first facilities to culture HIV from blood and semen samples while collaborating with Harvard Medical School.[54] The gay health centers of the 1970s also figured prominently among the recipient lists for the scant federal funding granted to AIDS research in the early years of the epidemic. The MAC Study, which Ostrow had lobbied for in 1983, hinged on the collaboration of numerous health centers, including the Howard Brown clinic and the Los Angeles Gay Community Services Center clinic. It also required the help of gay patients and community partnerships; nearly seven thousand men enrolled in the study in 1984. More than thirty years later, this study remains active, having produced more than 1,300 publications that have improved the understanding of AIDS and informed public health policy.[55] Representing only one of the research efforts that emanated from the gay health landscape of the 1970s to address the AIDS crisis, the MAC Study perfectly illuminates the collaborative methods, political backbone, and long-term importance of the gay medical infrastructure that gay health activists built in the 1970s.

The early and vigorous response to the AIDS crisis lays bare both the tremendous gains of 1970s health activism and the inevitable failings of medicine and public health when facing a new disease, particularly one that disproportionately affects socially and politically marginalized groups. The catastrophe of the early AIDS crisis should not eclipse the breadth and depth of the gay health networks of the 1970s. Rather, the calamity of those years and the lingering anger at ineffective leadership, slashed funding, and slow governmental response will only become starker and stronger through understanding what *did* exist. Gay health activists mounted the strongest and most meaningful responses to the early AIDS crisis, and they often did so out of overcrowded, underfunded, and slapdash facilities staffed by volunteers. The fact that the first gay people with AIDS in New England found the most informed health professionals and the broadest range of support services at the Fenway clinic, a basement clinic with an entrance in an alleyway off a small side street and an equally modest budget (rather than at any of Boston's world-class medical research institutions) speaks volumes about both the accomplishments of gay health activists of the 1970s and the incredibly dysfunctional national health response to AIDS in the early 1980s.

Gay health activists of the 1970s drew from a variety of social and political movements, deployed state funding and support in new and unintended ways, and created a multifaceted and strong gay medical infrastructure in the 1970s that reflected local politics while addressing common concerns of gay patients. Their efforts provided unprecedented improvements in the quality of health care gay patients could receive and made great strides toward creating an effective hepatitis B vaccine. The accomplishments of these activists reflect their passion as well as the needs of their patients. The early AIDS crisis again called upon the passion, network building, and determination to provide quality care and conduct meaningful research that had been the bedrock of the 1970s gay health movement.

AIDS AND THE STATE ENMESHED

Historical and popular views emphasize one of two aspects of the early AIDS crisis: state abandonment and outward hostility toward communities afflicted by AIDS or direct action protests such as those associated with ACT UP and the AIDS Memorial Quilt, which forced the attention of an uncaring and uneducated society. Certainly many examples provide a strong foundation for both of these narratives. Consider the October 1982 White House press briefing in which White House press secretary Larry Speakes called into question the sexuality of a journalist who asked a question about AIDS, evoking laughter from himself and the press corps.[1] Or, even more egregious and exemplary of governmental apathy, the simple fact that President Ronald Reagan, often dubbed "the Great Communicator," failed to publicly utter the word AIDS until September 1985, after more than five thousand American citizens had died of the disease. ACT UP protests frequently targeted government buildings with dramatic demonstrations, whether dumping ashes of loved ones on the White House lawn or storming the National Institutes of Health. These perspectives on the history of AIDS present a teleology, in which state abandonment resulted in activism. Moreover, these narratives emphasize antagonism and opposition between the state and gay communities.[2] In this way, the chapter on AIDS in the larger story of LGBTQ history plays out in a typical and unsurprising way that places LGBTQ communities at odds with the state, with one protesting the deficiencies of the other.

This book tells a different story of AIDS, and, perhaps even more significantly, of the relationship between gay community building and the state more broadly. In this narrative, the gay community already had a robust health network prior to the AIDS epidemic and the state was already deeply imbricated in that infrastructure. Moreover, the development of this landscape in the 1970s exemplified the neoliberal off-loading of the social safety net that has become a hallmark of the last sixty years in American history. From the perspective of these activists, their clinics, and the national gay health networks they cultivated, the relationship between gay people and the state is not one characterized by pure opposition or abandonment, but rather one of enmeshment.

As the state sought to address the nation's health disparities during the Great Society programs of the 1960s, it funneled funds to local community health clinics in an act of neoliberal compromise that neither offered the universal government-run health care those on the left wanted nor entirely removed the state from funding any health-care services as those on the right desired. These funds paved the way for a patchwork of services that often reflected the specific communities they served, and offered those seeking gay health services a clear pathway to creating them. The need for health services within gay communities drove activists and organizations to measure their (sometimes deeply held) political antagonism toward the state, seeking out ways to balance their politics with their need for services that state funding could and did make possible. Slowly and painfully over the course of a decade the need for and access to health services tempered the politics of clinics and organizations. This enmeshment process brought significant results for both the state and gay communities. For the state, a wide range of previously critical and organized activists were pacified, and simultaneously more effective public health interventions in the VD epidemic were carried out. In return, gay communities created much easier access to high-quality affordable medical care and effectively redefined notions of gay health in both the gay and the medical communities. Though its relationship with the state was often fraught, gay health activism simply would not have materialized as it did in the 1970s nor to the extent that it did without the state.

Even with the emergence of AIDS, the tectonic political shifts of 1981, and the reallocation of most public funds for gay health services, gay health activism fails to fit within the AIDS abandonment narrative. Without question, the cuts in funding hurt and diminished the potential for gay health activists' more meaningful medical responses to AIDS. However, gay health activism in the early AIDS crisis again highlights the enmeshment between the state and gay health services, most specifically in the organizations, networks, and research that state funding had helped create in the 1970s. The AIDS abandonment narrative recounts the important history of a government that turned its back on people with AIDS, who were often members of stigmatized minority groups. The history of gay health activism does not counter that history, nor does it diminish the powerful forms of activism that materialized in opposition to the state in the later half of the 1980s. Rather, it sheds light on activism in the immediate response to the early AIDS crisis and traces that activism (and the resultant services) to both the political groundings of activists and the relationships they had navigated with the state in the preceding decade. Gay health clinics, both built with the help of the state and increasingly forsaken by it, met the AIDS epidemic head-on, creating and offering the services that would eventually be spread out across multiple organizations in each city to address the crisis. They drew on their varied histories, political framings, understandings of gay health, savvy regarding government funding, network building, and information-disseminating techniques to serve as the very first frontline in the epidemic. The state could take away funding and support during the AIDS crisis, but it couldn't erase the networks, knowledge, and research of the 1970s.

This enmeshment with the state had significant implications for the gay health clinics' early AIDS response. Years of navigating state-funding processes had taught Dr. David Ostrow that pressuring Congress to fund the already approved MAC Study was the best chance of getting funding. When the Fenway clinic's Dr. Ken Mayer needed to report the first AIDS case in New England, he called the CDC researchers with whom he had a nearly decade-old working relationship, who would also be tasked with understanding and responding to AIDS. Clinic compliance with state regulations made clinics more appealing to outside funders and adept at grant writing (which would prove crucial as state funds evaporated throughout the 1980s). To be clear, I am not trying to argue that the state's response to the AIDS crisis was anything other than abysmal. Nor am I suggesting that gay clinics, without the state support they had cultivated over the 1970s, provided the best possible AIDS response. Ideally, the state would have maintained its strong relationship with gay community clinics, working in tandem and at full capacity to understand and contain the epidemic. Of course, that did not happen. Gay community clinics and activists faced the epidemic with only personal relationships with suddenly overburdened government insiders and some knowledge of political maneuvering, but very little of the state-funding support of the previous decade. However, the state unintentionally strengthened even this compromised response to the early crisis on the part of gay health clinics through the strong role it had played in their development in the 1970s.

The concept of enmeshment with the state matters in the history of AIDS in two major ways. First, it provides greater nuance, showcasing the important role of the state in creating gay services and institutions and complicating the purely oppositional narrative dominant in the literatures. And second, it recognizes the importance of the meaningful, though not always direct, activism of those who responded to AIDS from the very first cases. Founded in 1987, ACT UP and its contemporaries offer tremendous insight into the intersection of health, politics, and sexuality in the final years of the decade, and embody such rage and desperation as to suggest that they were the first political responses to AIDS (from the gay community and beyond). The tactics and impact of ACT UP have garnered the most significant scholarly attention to date in the still nascent field of AIDS history, unintentionally threatening to erase or diminish earlier modes of activism.[3] However, in offering education, fighting for funding, creating palliative and support services, and trying various treatments, gay health activists housed within gay health clinics attest that the political response to AIDS occurred from the very start of the epidemic. Their activism was political in that it drew on a myriad of political tactics and legacies linked to individual clinics' origins that went back more than a decade, demanded more from the state, and played out in specifically gay clinics that aligned themselves with the very communities that bore the brunt of AIDS stigma. Though not as dramatic or emotional as a die-in protest or the unfurling of a quilt the size of the Mall in Washington, these early forms of activism existed years before the first ACT UP meetings in 1987 and shaped the early AIDS response and trajectory in meaningful ways on personal, political, and medical levels. And unlike the activism of the final years of the decade, they did so in large part because of the networks and services built (with the help of the state) before AIDS.

Beyond the ever-growing field of AIDS history, the concept of enmeshment with the state appears valuable and thought provoking for the larger field of LGBTQ studies. If the late 1970s was the high-water mark for the entanglement between the state and gay health, our current historical moment is one in which a many LGBTQ communities have willingly (in fact, victoriously) interwoven themselves with the state. Whether through same-sex marriage, the inclusion of transgender people in the military, or even the governmental debates on gender-less bathrooms in public spaces, the state and LGBTQ communities are intertwined in historically significant ways and to historically deep extents. What is gained, lost, and risked as a result of this enmeshment? Have LGBTQ communities bought into a neoliberal notion of citizenship in a way that will prove detrimental to the very sexual and gender identities to which they ascribe? Have they, like the gay health activists of the 1970s, tempered their politics in exchange for these rights? What implications does this relationship to the state have for intersectionality and the whitewashing of LGBTQ politics? Is the winning of specific state protections and rights the best (or only) political path forward in securing freedom for all members of the LGBTQ communities? These are the very questions driving scholarship on the "homonormative turn," or, as Lisa Duggan defines it, "a politics that does not contest dominant heteronormative assumptions and institutions, but upholds and sustains them, while promising the possibility of a demobilized gay constituency and a privatized, depoliticized gay culture anchored in domesticity and consumption."[4] This history of gay health activism frames, contextualizes, and historicizes the homonormative turn that Duggan, David Eng, Jasbir Puar, Dean Spade, and others have articulated.[5]

These clinics are the early harbingers of the full-throttle homonormative turn of the 1990s. They provide an opportunity to trace the roots of 1990s corporate-sponsored activism and gay capitalism back two decades earlier into small gay nonprofits thinking strategically about fund-ability and making seemingly minor political compromises that compounded over time. Eventually these clinics became part of a larger backdrop and foundation for homonormativity as Duggan understands it, privileging wealth, whiteness, gender conformity, and liberal, rather than radical, politics. Of course, the clinics of the 1970s and early 1980s merely understood their actions as making the necessary decisions to meet the sexual health needs of gay patients in the context of capitalist health care and a fragmented welfare state. To be clear, I am not begrudging them their choices, as many examples of closed clinics suggest that they were often decisions of survival, of providing services or not. However, connecting the dots between the experiences of these clinics and their activists and the evolution of gay politics and rise of homonormativism in the 1990s and beyond further demonstrates their historical importance.

LGBTQ health activism is not relegated to the past. Rather, it remains a potent political catalyst for organizing, as patients and health-care providers still push to erase the significant health disparities that linger in and between these communities—a struggle that has grown slightly easier if also much more complex. The individuals, clinics, and national networks of the 1970s continue to lead this effort, with the help of a new generation, spurred by the AIDS crisis, the continued growth of LGBTQ institutions, and often with greater funding and support from the state. They continue to grapple with their political ideals and the limits posed by the state in addressing LGBTQ health needs, offering another vantage point from which to view (reluctant? incomplete?) homonormativity at an institutional level. Just as in the 1970s, gay health activists and the state continue to push one another onto uncomfortable footing as, for example, clinics seek to address the health needs of individuals who are not fully recognized by government bodies like the CDC (as was the case for women with AIDS before 1993 or for trans people before 2013).[6] Millions of dollars of state grants support the cutting-edge research at many of these facilities, but sometimes at the cost of trust and inclusion of some subsets of the LGBTQ communities that reflect racial, gender, age, and economic divisions that already existed both within the organizations and the communities they serve. In many ways, the gay health clinics of the 1970s have become so complex over the last forty years that to fully trace the role of the state, politics, and the dissemination of services among various LGBTQ communities would require another, different book. However, these organizations stand as cultural and medical institutions in their cities and nationally, embodying the homonormative turn while also often situated on the frontlines of the next LGBTQ health issue that challenges norms, recasts medical discourse, and renegotiates the concept of health both within and beyond the LGBTQ communities. These clinics undoubtedly will continue the tradition they started in the 1970s as gay health clinics: to be important sites of political negotiation between sexuality, the state, and health.

Introduction

1. Gary Chichester, interview by author, May 19, 2007.

2. Ibid.

3. Centers for Disease Control and Prevention, *Tracking the Hidden Epidemics: Trends in STDs in the United States 2000* (2000), http://www.cdc.gov/std/trends2000/Trends2000.pdf, booklet.

4. Chuck Renslow, interview by author, August 14, 2007.

5. S. Gold and I. L. Neufeld, "A Learning Approach to the Treatment of Homosexuality," *Behaviour Research and Therapy* 3 (1965): 201–4; G. R. Peberdy, "Homosexuality and the Law," *Medico-legal Journal* 33 (1965): 29–34; K. Freund, "On the Problem of Male Homosexuality," *Review of Czechoslovak Medicine* 11 (1965): 11–17; T. McCracken, "Homosexuality," *Journal of the College of General Practitioners* 9, no. S1 (1965): 16–25; Y. R. De Monch, "A Clinical Type of Male Homosexuality," *International Journal of Psychoanalysis* 46 (1965): 218–25; S. C. Mason et al., "Homosexuality: A Medico-legal Problem," *Journal—Michigan State Medical Society* 60 (1961): 635–38; O. S. English, "A Primer on Homosexuality," *GP* 7, no. 4 (1953): 55–60; K. M. Bowman and B. Engle, "The Problem of Homosexuality," *Journal of Social Hygiene* 39, no. 1 (1953): 2–16.

6. C. B. Golin, "MDs Assess Problems in Treating Gays," *IMPACT* section of *American Medical News,* October 27, 1978.

7. The diseases that posed the greatest threat to the gay male community at this time were syphilis, hepatitis, gonorrhea, and herpes, along with many other less serious ailments. Many of the STDs prevalent have easily missed initial symptoms, but all have very serious, potentially deadly long-term effects. Syphilis, also called the great masquerader, is infamous for imitating other nonsexually transmitted diseases, but can culminate in skin sores, respiratory problems, and insanity. Gonorrhea is often symptom-less, especially when in the throat, but ultimately makes urination excruciating and can spread into the blood stream, becoming life-threatening. Hepatitis often resembles a cold or flu, but eventually attacks the liver.

8. Golin, "MDs Assess Problems"; David Ostrow et al., "Epidemiology of Gonorrhea Infections in Gay Men," *Journal of Homosexuality* 5, no. 3 (1980): 285–89; David Ostrow and Dale Shaskey, "The VD Epidemiological Experience of the Howard Brown Memorial

Clinic of Chicago" (paper presented at the Annual Meeting of the American Public Health Association, Miami Beach, Florida, 1976); David Ostrow, "An Epidemiological Study of Venereal Disease among Male Homosexuals: A Research Proposal," 1975, David Ostrow Papers, box 5, STD Archives folder, GH; L. Dardick, "Openness Between Gay People and Health Professionals and Its Effect on Quality of Care" (paper presented at the Annual Meeting of the American Public Health Association, New York, November 1979).

9. Syphilis was more than two times more common among gay men than in the heterosexual population. Gonorrhea was also slightly more common, as was hepatitis B. U.S. Department of Health, Education and Welfare Center for Disease Control, "Figures and Tables for 'Profile of the Gay Std Patient,'" 1976, WLPC; Alfred Baker, "Chronic Type B Hepatitis in Gay Men: Experience with Patients Referred from the Howard Brown Memorial Clinic to the University of Chicago," *Journal of Homosexuality* 5, no. 3 (1980): 311–15; Marshall Schreeder et al., "Epidemiology of Hepatitis B Infection in Gay Men," *Journal of Homosexuality* 5, no. 3 (1980): 307–10; William W. Darrow et al., "The Gay Report on Sexually Transmitted Diseases," *American Journal of Public Health* 71, no. 9 (1981): 1004–1011.

10. Renslow, interview.

11. Jonathan Bell, *California Crucible: The Forging of Modern American Liberalism*, Politics and Culture in Modern America (Philadelphia: University of Pennsylvania Press, 2012); Bell, *The Liberal State on Trial: The Cold War and American Politics in the Truman Years*, Columbia Studies in Contemporary American History (New York: Columbia University Press, 2004); Jonathan Bell and Timothy Stanley, *Making Sense of American Liberalism* (Urbana: University of Illinois Press, 2012); Emily K. Hobson, *Lavender and Red: Liberation and Solidarity in the Gay and Lesbian Left* (Oakland: University of California Press, 2016); Tamar W. Carroll, *Mobilizing New York: AIDS, Antipoverty, and Feminist Activism* (Chapel Hill: University of North Carolina Press, 2015); Timothy Stewart-Winter, *Queer Clout: Chicago and the Rise of Gay Politics*, Politics and Culture in Modern America (Philadelphia: University of Pennsylvania Press, 2016); Jennifer Brier, *Infectious Ideas: U.S. Political Responses to the AIDS Crisis* (Chapel Hill: University of North Carolina Press, 2009); Robert O. Self, *All in the Family: The Realignment of American Democracy since the 1960s* (New York: Hill and Wang, 2012).

12. Siobhan B. Somerville, *Queering the Color Line: Race and the Invention of Homosexuality in American Culture* (Durham, N.C.: Duke University Press, 2000); Ian Baldwin, "Family, Housing, and the Political Geography of Gay Liberation in Los Angeles County, 1960–1986" (PhD diss., University of Nevada, Las Vegas, 2016); Margot Canaday, *The Straight State: Sexuality and Citizenship in Twentieth-Century America* (Princeton, N.J.: Princeton University Press, 2009); Eithne Luibhéid, *Entry Denied: Controlling Sexuality at the Border* (Minneapolis: University of Minnesota Press, 2002); Martin Meeker, "The Queerly Disadvantaged and the Making of San Francisco's War on Poverty, 1964–1967," *Pacific Historical Review* 81, no. 1 (2012): 21–59.

13. A growing body of literature explores that relationship between the Great Society

and health programs. See Annelise Orleck and Lisa Gayle Hazirjian, *The War on Poverty: A New Grassroots History, 1964–1980* (Athens: University of Georgia Press, 2011); John Dittmer, *The Good Doctors: The Medical Committee for Human Rights and the Struggle for Social Justice in Health Care* (New York: Bloomsbury Press, 2009); Jonathan Engel, *Poor People's Medicine: Medicaid and American Charity Care since 1965* (Durham, N.C.: Duke University Press, 2006).

14. Ronald P. Formisano, *Boston Against Busing: Race, Class, and Ethnicity in the 1960s and 1970s* (Chapel Hill: University of North Carolina Press, 2004); Heather Ann Thompson, *Speaking Out: Activism and Protest in the 1960s and 1970s* (Boston: Prentice Hall, 2009); Jefferson Cowie, *Stayin' Alive: The 1970s and the Last Days of the Working Class* (New York: New Press, 2010); Bruce J. Schulman and Julian E. Zelizer, *Rightward Bound: Making America Conservative in the 1970s* (Cambridge, Mass.: Harvard University Press, 2008); Edward D. Berkowitz, *Something Happened: A Political and Cultural Overview of the Seventies* (New York: Columbia University Press, 2006); Peter N. Carroll, *It Seemed Like Nothing Happened: America in the 1970s* (New Brunswick, N.J.: Rutgers University Press, 2000); Rick Perlstein, *Nixonland: The Rise of a President and the Fracturing of America* (New York: Scribner, 2008); Bernard von Bothmer, *Framing the Sixties: The Use and Abuse of a Decade from Ronald Reagan to George W. Bush* (Amherst: University of Massachusetts Press, 2009).

15. Rebecca Chalker, "Lesbian Health Care," in *Sourcebook on Lesbian/Gay Healthcare* (New York: New York City Health Department, 1984), 92.

16. Other examples of this trend include Stewart-Winter, *Queer Clout*; Julio Capó Jr. "Queering Mariel: Mediating Cold War Foreign Policy and US Citizenship Among Cuba's Homosexual Exile Community, 1978–1994," *Journal of American Ethnic History* 29, no. 4 (2010): 78–106; Kwame A. Holmes, "Chocolate to Rainbow City: The Dialectics of Black and Gay Community Formation in Postwar Washington, DC, 1946–1978" (PhD diss., University of Illinois at Urbana-Champaign, 2011); Stewart Van Cleve, *Land of 10,000 Loves* (Minneapolis: University of Minnesota Press, 2012).

17. David Scondras, interview by author, January 6, 2001.

18. The project was eventually scrapped after a large and sustained community protest of which the Black Panther Clinic was a part. See Alan Lupo, Frank Colcord, and Edmund P. Fowler, *Rites of Way: The Politics of Transportation in Boston and the U.S. City* (Boston: Little, Brown, 1971).

19. Scondras, interview.

20. Ibid.

21. "Gay Medical Students," *Chicago Gay Crusader*, May 1973. Ostrow had a separate line installed in his apartment explicitly for these calls.

22. David Ostrow, interview by author, March 23, 2007.

23. Thomas Martorelli, *For People, Not for Profit: A History of Fenway Health's First Forty Years* (Bloomington, Ind.: AuthorHouse, 2012).

24. The Los Angeles Gay Community Services Center Archives are now processed and the ONE Archive is now affiliated with the University of Southern California.

25. David Carter, *Stonewall: The Riots That Sparked the Gay Revolution* (New York: St. Martin's Press, 2004); Martin B. Duberman, *Stonewall* (New York: Dutton, 1993); Chichester, interview.

26. Allan Bérubé, *Coming Out Under Fire: The History of Gay Men and Women in World War Two* (New York: Free Press, 1990); John D'Emilio, *Sexual Politics, Sexual Communities: The Making of a Homosexual Minority in the United States, 1940–1970*, 2nd ed. (Chicago: University of Chicago Press, 1998); Lillian Faderman and Stuart Timmons, *Gay L.A.: A History of Sexual Outlaws, Power Politics, and Lipstick Lesbians* (New York: Basic Books, 2006); David K. Johnson, *The Lavender Scare: The Cold War Persecution of Gays and Lesbians in the Federal Government* (Chicago: University of Chicago Press, 2004). Of course, homosexuals of previous periods also created their own social spaces, communities, and cultures, but the postwar period marked an era of growing political awareness and activism on the basis of sexuality for gays and lesbians. On earlier sexual communities, see Lillian Faderman, *Odd Girls and Twilight Lovers: A History of Lesbian Life in Twentieth-Century America*, Between Men—Between Women (New York: Columbia University Press, 1991); Elizabeth Kennedy and Madeline Davis, *Boots of Leather, Slippers of Gold* (New York: Penguin Books, 1994); George Chauncey, *Gay New York: Gender, Urban Culture, and the Makings of the Gay Male World, 1890–1940* (New York: Basic Books, 1994); John Howard, *Men Like That: A Southern Queer History* (Chicago: University of Chicago Press, 1999); Kevin Mumford, *Interzones: Black/White Sex Districts in Chicago and New York in the Early Twentieth Century* (New York: Columbia University Press, 1997); Nan Alamilla Boyd, *Wide-Open Town: A History of Queer San Francisco to 1965* (Berkeley: University of California Press, 2003); C. Todd White, *Pre-Gay L.A.: A Social History of the Movement for Homosexual Rights* (Urbana: University of Illinois Press, 2009); Chad C. Heap, *Slumming: Sexual and Racial Encounters in American Nightlife, 1885–1940* (Chicago: University of Chicago Press, 2009); Daniel Hurewitz, *Bohemian Los Angeles and the Making of Modern Politics* (Berkeley: University of California Press, 2007); Marcia Gallo, *Different Daughters: A History of the Daughters of Bilitis and the Rise of the Lesbian Rights Movement* (Emeryville, Calif.: Seal Press, 2007).

27. On the founding, actions, and politics of these groups, see D'Emilio, *Sexual Politics, Sexual Communities*; Stewart-Winter, *Queer Clout*.

28. On the 1960s, see Rebecca E. Klatch, *A Generation Divided: The New Left, the New Right, and the 1960s* (Berkeley: University of California Press, 1999); Edmund Lindop and Margaret J. Goldstein, *America in the 1960s* (Minneapolis: Twenty-First Century Books, 2009); Bothmer, *Framing the Sixties*; Formisano, *Boston Against Busing*; Maurice Isserman and Michael Kazin, *America Divided: The Civil War of the 1960s*, 2nd ed. (New York: Oxford University Press, 2003). On the sexual revolution, see Beth L. Bailey, *Sex in the Heartland* (Cambridge, Mass.: Harvard University Press, 1999).

29. Belinda Baldwin, "L.A., 1/1/67: The Black Cat Riots," *Gay and Lesbian Review Worldwide* 13, no. 2 (2006): 28–30; *Screaming Queens: The Riot at Compton's Cafeteria*, directed by Victor Silverman and Susan Stryker (2005; San Francisco: KQED Television Frameline, 2006), DVD.

30. See Stewart-Winter, *Queer Clout*; Marc Stein, *City of Sisterly and Brotherly Loves: Lesbian and Gay Philadelphia, 1945–1972* (Philadelphia: Temple University Press, 2004); Faderman and Timmons, *Gay L.A.*; Terence Kissack, "Freaking Fag Revolutionaries: New York's Gay Liberation Front, 1969–1971," *Radical History Review* 62, no. 44–57 (1995): 104–34; Karla Jay, *Tales of the Lavender Menace: A Memoir of Liberation* (New York: Basic Books, 1999); Horacio N. Roque Ramirez, "'That's My Place!': Negotiating Racial, Sexual, and Gender Politics in San Francisco's Gay Latino Alliance, 1975–1983," *Journal of the History of Sexuality* 12, no. 2 (2003): 224–58; Daneel Buring, "Gay Activism Behind the Magnolia Curtain: The Memphis Gay Coalition, 1979–1991," *Journal of Homosexuality* 32, no. 1 (1996): 113–35; Elizabeth A. Armstrong, *Forging Gay Identities: Organizing Sexuality in San Francisco, 1950–1994* (Chicago: University of Chicago Press, 2002).

31. Alexandra Chasin, *Selling Out: The Gay and Lesbian Movement Goes to Market* (New York: St. Martin's Press, 2000); Anne Enke, *Finding the Movement: Sexuality, Contested Space, and Feminist Activism*, Radical Perspectives (Durham, N.C.: Duke University Press, 2007); Anne M. Valk, *Radical Sisters: Second-Wave Feminism and Black Liberation in Washington, D.C.* (Urbana: University of Illinois Press, 2008); Stephanie Gilmore and Elizabeth Kaminski, "A Part and Apart: Lesbian and Straight Feminist Activists Negotiate Identity in a Second-Wave Organization," *Journal of the History of Sexuality* 16, no. 1 (2007): 95–113. In feminism, see Kimberly Springer, *Living for the Revolution: Black Feminist Organizations, 1968–1980* (Durham, N.C.: Duke University Press, 2005); Jo Reger, *Different Wavelengths: Studies of the Contemporary Women's Movement* (New York: Routledge, 2005).

32. Gays and lesbians were far from the only ones to challenge medical authority and the way in which medicine often reinforced political oppression and marginalization during this period. Duane F. Stroman, *The Disability Rights Movement: From Deinstitutionalization to Self-Determination* (Lanham, Md.: University Press of America, 2003); Jennifer Nelson, *Women of Color and the Reproductive Rights Movement* (New York: New York University Press, 2003); Sandra Morgen, *Into Our Own Hands: The Women's Health Movement in the United States, 1969–1990* (New Brunswick, N.J.: Rutgers University Press, 2002); Sharon N. Barnartt and Richard K. Scotch, *Disability Protests: Contentious Politics, 1970–1999* (Washington, D.C.: Gallaudet University Press, 2001).

33. Kathleen Cleaver and George Katsiaficas, eds., *Liberation, Imagination, and the Black Panther Party: A New Look at the Panthers and Their Legacy* (New York: Routledge, 2001); Huey P. Newton et al., *The Black Panther Leaders Speak: Huey P. Newton, Bobby Seale, Eldridge Cleaver, and Company Speak Out Through the Black Panther Party's Official Newspaper* (Metuchen, N.J.: Scarecrow Press, 1976); David Hilliard, ed., *The Black Panther Party: Service to the People Programs* (Albuquerque: University of New Mexico Press, 2008); Alondra Nelson, *Body and Soul: The Black Panther Party and the Fight Against Medical Discrimination* (Minneapolis: University of Minnesota Press, 2011).

34. Nelson, *Women of Color and the Reproductive Rights Movement*; "'Hold Your Head up and Stick out Your Chin': Community Health and Women's Health in Mound

Bayou, Mississippi," *NWSA Journal* 17, no. 1 (2005): 99–118; Morgen, *Into Our Own Hands*; Elena Gutierrez et al., *Undivided Rights: Women of Color Organizing for Reproductive Rights* (Boston: South End, 2004); Jane Lawrence, "The Indian Health Service and the Sterilization of Native American Women," *American Indian Quarterly* 24, no. 3 (2000): 400–419; Abraham Bergman et al., "A Political History of the Indian Health Service," *Millbank Quarterly* 77, no. 4 (1999): 571–604; Wendy Kline, *Bodies of Knowledge: Sexuality, Reproduction, and Women's Health in the Second Wave* (Chicago: University of Chicago Press, 2010).

35. Stroman, *The Disability Rights Movement*; Ruth Wilson Gilmore, *Golden Gulag: Prisons, Surplus, Crisis, and Opposition in Globalizing California*, American Crossroads (Berkeley: University of California Press, 2007); Barnartt and Scotch, *Disability Protests*; Gerald N. Grob, *From Asylum to Community: Mental Health Policy in Modern America* (Princeton, N.J.: Princeton University Press, 1991).

36. Rosemary Stevens, *In Sickness and in Wealth: American Hospitals in the Twentieth Century* (Baltimore: Johns Hopkins University Press, 1999); Stevens, *The Public-Private Health Care State: Essays on the History of American Health Care Policy* (New Brunswick, N.J.: Transaction Publishers, 2007); Rosemary Stevens, Charles E. Rosenberg, and Lawton R. Burns, *History and Health Policy in the United States: Putting the Past Back In* (New Brunswick, N.J.: Rutgers University Press, 2006); Engel, *Poor People's Medicine*; James H. Jones and Tuskegee Institute, *Bad Blood: The Tuskegee Syphilis Experiment* (New York: Free Press, 1993).

37. W. Rottersman, "Homosexuality," *Journal of the Medical Association of Georgia* 50 (1961): 245–46; Mason et al., "Homosexuality"; B. S. Aaronson and H. R. Grumpelt, "Homosexuality and Some MMPI Measures of Masculinity-Femininity," *Journal of Clinical Psychology* 17 (1961): 245–47; Bowman and Engle, "The Problem of Homosexuality." On the history of the relationship between medicine and homosexuality, see Jennifer Terry, *An American Obsession: Science, Medicine, and Homosexuality in Modern Society* (Chicago: University of Chicago Press, 1999); Ronald Bayer, *Homosexuality and American Psychiatry: The Politics of Diagnosis* (Princeton, N.J.: Princeton University Press, 1987); Steven Epstein, "Sexualizing Governance and Medicalising Identities: The Emergence of 'State-Centered' LGBT Health Politics in the United States," *Sexualities* 6, no. 2 (2003): 131–71; Jack Drescher and Joseph P. Merlino, *American Psychiatry and Homosexuality: An Oral History* (New York: Harrington Park Press, 2007).

38. On gays and lesbians coming out in the medical field, see "I Am a Lesbian Health Care Worker," 1976, box 64, Boston Women's Health Book Collective Papers, Countway Medical Library, Harvard University, Boston; Howard Harrison, "Straight Talk from a Gay Doctor," *New Physician*, 1974, 34–36; Chris Coste, "Gay Doctors Edging out of the Closet," *New Physician*, 1974, 30–33; Dittmer, *The Good Doctors*; Howard Brown, *Familiar Faces, Hidden Lives: The Story of Homosexual Men in America Today* (New York: Harcourt Brace Jovanovich, 1976).

39. Drescher and Merlino, *American Psychiatry and Homosexuality*; Bayer, *Homosexuality and American Psychiatry*.

40. Brier, *Infectious Ideas*; Deborah B. Gould, *Moving Politics: Emotion and Act Up's Fight Against AIDS* (Chicago: University of Chicago Press, 2009); Jonathan Engel, *The Epidemic: A Global History of AIDS* (New York: Smithsonian Books/Collins, 2006); Eric E. Rofes, *Dry Bones Breathe: Gay Men Creating Post-AIDS Identities and Cultures*, Haworth Gay & Lesbian Studies (New York: Haworth Press, 1998); Cindy Patton, *Sex and Germs: The Politics of AIDS* (Boston: South End Press, 1985); Cathy J. Cohen, *The Boundaries of Blackness: AIDS and the Breakdown of Black Politics* (Chicago: University of Chicago Press, 1999).

41. Bonnie Lefkowitz, *Community Health Centers: A Movement and the People Who Made It Happen*, Critical Issues in Health and Medicine (New Brunswick, N.J.: Rutgers University Press, 2007).

42. John Kenneth Galbraith, *The Affluent Society* (Boston: Houghton Mifflin, 1958); Michael Harrington, *The Other America: Poverty in the United States* (New York: Macmillan, 1962); Engel, *Poor People's Medicine*; Stevens, *The Public-Private Health Care State*; Stevens, Rosenberg, and Burns, *History and Health Policy in the United States*; Jill S. Quadagno, *One Nation, Uninsured: Why the U.S. Has No National Health Insurance* (New York: Oxford University Press, 2006); Marie Gottschalk, *The Shadow Welfare State: Labor, Business, and the Politics of Health-Care in the United States* (Ithaca, N.Y.: ILR Press, 2000).

Chapter 1

1. "Mission and History," Fenway Center, http://www.fenwaycdc.org/about-us/history, accessed September 25, 2008; Benjamin Jones v. James T. Lynn, No. 73-1057 (1st Cir. 1973).

2. David Scondras, interview by author, January 6, 2001; Fenway Community Health Center, "Opening New Doors . . . 20 Years of Making a Difference: An Oral History of the Fenway Community Health Center," ed. Kirk Kinder (Boston: Fenway Community Health Center, 1991). Booklet.

3. Fenway Community Health Center, "Opening New Doors . . ."; Scondras, interview.

4. Karla Rideout, interview by author, July 12, 2007; Fenway Community Health Center, "Opening New Doors . . ."

5. Rideout, interview.

6. Ibid.

7. Fenway Community Health Center, "Opening New Doors . . ."

8. Lenny Alberts, interview by author, July 11, 2007.

9. Bureau of the Census, *1970 Census of Population and Housing: Census Tracts Boston, Massachusetts Standard Metropolitan Statistical Area* (Washington, D.C.: U.S. Government Printing Office, 1972). This number is significantly higher when focused solely upon children or the elderly. The actual numbers fluctuate slightly depending on how "poverty" is defined and calculated. For a more in-depth explanation, see Engel, *Poor People's Medicine*, 5–7. Harrington, *The Other America*, 180–91.

10. Ira Wyman, "Boston's Symphony Rd.: A Medley of Fires, Drugs, Decay, and Fear," *New York Times*, October 25, 1977, 18. In fact, according to the 1970 census, over 55 percent of those living in the Fenway were between the ages of eighteen and twenty-four, while that age range made up only 12 percent of the larger Boston population. Over 40 percent of area residents were college students.

11. Alberts, interview.

12. Ibid.

13. Scondras, interview.

14. There was also a women's health night on Thursdays. The clinic location also served as home to the cooperative day-care center, and on Saturday morning it provided a venue for the showing of Saturday morning movies for the children of the neighborhood, reflecting the closeness of the community and the centrality of this location in nurturing the strong identity of the community.

15. Theresa Tobin and Stephen Brophy, joint interview by author, September 17, 2007.

16. Ibid.

17. Michael Vance, interview by author, December 13, 2007.

18. Scondras, interview.

19. Ibid.

20. "Fenway Community Health Center Proposal to Otherfund, Inc.," December 15, 1974, box 1, series II, folder 16, Laura McMurry Collection, #17, HPA, 3–4.

21. Alberts, interview.

22. Fenway Community Health Center, "Opening New Doors . . ."

23. Alberts, interview; Tobin and Brophy, joint interview.

24. Also to a lesser extent, the Fenway clinic offered services for lesbians. Given the limited understanding of the specific needs of the lesbian community, all the services for lesbians were offered under the auspices of women's health. Tobin and Brophy, joint interview.

25. At the time, employers had access to employee medical insurance claims, thus VD testing and treatment could lead employers to uncover closeted employees.

26. Alberts, interview.

27. Vance, interview.

28. Donald Kilhefner, interview by author, October 31, 2007.

29. Ibid.

30. John Platania, "John Platania's Recorded Impressions of the Gay Community Services Center," June 19, 1991, audiocassette tape, box 236, MKP.

31. Kilhefner, interview.

32. "Weekly Calendar of Events at the Gay Community Services Center," 1973, box 104-101, GCSCP.

33. "The Center Purpose, Objectives, and Facilities," 1971, the Gay and Lesbian Community Services Center Subject File, OA; "Articles of Incorporation of the Gay Community Services Center," 1971, box 4, folder 2, MKP.

34. Kilhefner, interview.

35. On radical gay activism and gay liberation in Los Angeles during this period, see Moira Rachel Kenney, *Mapping Gay L.A.: The Intersection of Place and Politics* (Philadelphia: Temple University Press, 2001); Faderman and Timmons, *Gay L.A*; Yolanda Retter, "On the Side of Angels: Lesbian Activism in Los Angeles, 1970–1990" (PhD diss., University of New Mexico, 1999); Bell, *California Crucible*.

36. "Matching Activities to Needs of the Oppressed Paper," n.d., box 243, folder 1, MKP.

37. "The Center Purpose, Objectives, and Facilities."

38. "Gay Community Center Opens," 1971, box 104-113, GCSCP.

39. The Gay Community Services Center was the first organization in the country with the word "gay" in its name to gain 501(c)(3) tax exemption status, a process that required much fighting on the part of center activists and representatives. "Milton Cormy to the Gay Community Services Center, Regarding Tax Exempt Status of the Gay Community Services Center, 9 August," 1974, box 2, folder 4, MKP.

40. Kilhefner, interview.

41. Bell, *California Crucible*; Faderman and Timmons, *Gay L.A*; D'Emilio, *Sexual Politics, Sexual Communities*.

42. As a result, the Gay VD Clinic kept very detailed records of case contacts, numbers of new cases of venereal diseases, treatments, etc. "Evaluation of the Men's Clinic Performance November, 1974 through April," 1975, box 104-104, GCSCP.

43. Programs designed to address substance abuse within the gay community was another instance in which the state and gay concepts of health coincided with one another. "Letter to Josette Escamilla-Mondanaro, Regarding Funding for Substance Abuse Treatment Program at the Gay Community Services Center, 15 November," 1976, box 2, folder 4, MKP; "A Proposal for Funding for the Substance Abuse Treatment Program at the Gay Community Services Center," n.d., box 242, MKP.

44. "Press Release Announcing Clinic Opening, 11 October," 1972, box 104-101, GCSCP.

45. A generous inheritance allowed Teller to donate much of his time during the clinic's early stage. Once the clinic was fairly self-contained and running smoothly, he took a job at a local hospital. Teller had stopped briefly in Los Angeles and met with Kilhefner and Kight while on his way from working with the Centers for Disease Control in West Africa to San Francisco, where he hoped to start a gay health clinic. Despite Kilhefner and Kight's best efforts to persuade him to stay in Los Angeles and open up a clinic at the recently opened Gay Community Services Center, Teller was determined to go to San Francisco, only to realize within a few short months that the gay community in Los Angeles was much more organized and conducive to providing medical services to the gay community. Upon his return to Los Angeles, Teller agreed to share his license and liability insurance with the center and along with Kilhefner and Kight set to transforming a portion of the Wilshire house into a working clinic. Benjamin Teller, interview by author, November 1, 2007.

46. Teller, interview.

47. Ibid.

48. "The Gay Community Services Center Medical Program Staff Recruitment," 1974, box 104-101, GCSCP.

49. Teller, interview.

50. Ibid.

51. "'Don't Give Him Anything but Love' Poster," n.d., box 104-103, GCSCP; "Before It's Too Late: Learn About VD," n.d., box 104-101, GCSCP; "Venereal Disease Pamphlet," n.d., box 104-101, GCSCP; "'What Does Epidemiology Mean to You and to the Gay Community?' Handout," n.d., box 104-101, GCSCP.

52. Teller, interview.

53. "History and Objectives of the Gay Community Services Center," 1976, box 104-114, GCSCP; "Explanation of Programs and Other Services Available at the Gay Community Services Center for Grant and Funding Proposals," 1978, box 104-101, GCSCP; "Commentary on the 1974 Financial Report for the Gay Community Services Center, 31 December," 1974, box 104-113, GCSCP.

54. "Preliminary Financial Statements for Fiscal Year Ending December 31," 1976, box 104-114, GCSCP; "Gay Community Services Center Quarterly Report—31 March," 1972, Gay Community Services Center Collection, MA.

55. Sharon Raphael, interview by author, December 11, 2007.

56. "Memorandum Regarding Clinic Relocation & Licensing, 29 April," 1975, box 104-103, GCSCP.

57. "Explanation of Programs and Other Services," 1978, box 104-101, GCSCP.

58. "Introduction and Historical Perspective for the Gay Community Services Center," 1976, box 251, folder 5, MKC, 1–12; "Preliminary Financial Statements," 1976, box 104-114, GCSCP; "History and Objectives," 1976, box 104-114, GCSCP.

59. "Introduction and Historical Perspective," 1976, box 251, folder 5, MKC, 14.

60. "Fact Sheet," 1978, box 104-103, GCSCP.

61. Ostrow, interview.

62. Ibid.

63. Ibid.

64. Ibid.

65. Ibid.

66. Ibid.

67. "Gay Horizons Handout," 1974, David Ostrow Papers, GH.

68. "Press Release on V.D. Testing Services," 1974, David Ostrow Papers, GH.

69. Ibid.

70. Ken Mayer, interview by author, July 11, 2007.

71. "HBMC 25th Anniversary Timeline/Pamphlet," 1999, Howard Brown Memorial Clinic Papers, GH.

72. Ostrow, interview.

73. Mayer, interview.

74. Marcia Chambers, "Ex-City Official Says He's a Homosexual," *New York Times*, October 3, 1973, 1.

75. Beyond becoming a symbol of gay health activism, Brown became a hero and activist for the gay community at large, founding the National Gay Task Force. Brown, *Familiar Faces, Hidden Lives*.

76. "Howard Brown Memorial Clinic Quarterly Report," 1975, WLPC.

77. Ostrow, interview.

78. Ibid.

79. "Meeting of the Board of Directors of the Clinic, May 25," 1975, box 5, Board Meeting Minutes Folder, Howard Brown Memorial Clinic Papers, GH.

80. Ostrow, "An Epidemiological Study of Venereal Disease"; Ostrow, "Epidemiology of Gonorrhea Infections"; David Ostrow and Dale Shaskey, "The Experience of the Howard Brown Memorial Clinic of Chicago with Sexually Transmitted Diseases," *Sexually Transmitted Diseases* 4, no. 2 (1977): 53–55.

81. Center on Halsted, "Center on Halsted Organizational Timeline," http://www.centeronhalsted.org/cohhistory.html, accessed April 12, 2011.

Chapter 2

1. The Fenway Park baseball stadium opened on the neighborhood's northern border in 1912, the Boston Museum of Fine Arts moved to the neighborhood in 1909, the New England Conservatory of Music moved to the neighborhood in 1903 from its previous South End location, and Harvard Medical School moved to its current location in the neighborhood in 1906.

2. Boston Redevelopment Authority, *Fenway Urban Renewal Plan* (1965), 7, http://www.fenwaycdc.org/about-us/history, accessed September 25, 2008.

3. Activists also addressed the neighborhood's arson problem, which had resulted in more than two dozen fires, claimed the homes of hundreds, and killed five, by founding the Symphony Tenants Organizing Project (STOP) in September 1976. The organization conducted clandestine research on the properties and owners affected by the fires resulting in 121 indictments against 33 people relating to 35 fires destroying property valued at $6 million, the largest arson-for-profit ring ever uncovered. Among those implicated were retired policemen, firemen, real estate brokers, lawyers, lenders, public adjusters, and other businessmen. Tobin and Brophy, interview; John Cullen, "Over 100 Probed in $2 Million Arson Scheme," *Boston Globe*, September 22, 1977, 1, 10; Michael Knight, "Arson Arrests in Massachusetts Laid to Victims' Detective Work," *New York Times*, October 19, 1977, A16; Joseph Egelhof, "Arson Ring Crackdown Is Victory for Tenants," *Chicago Tribune*, October 23, 1977, 1, 10; "22 Seized in Boston in Arson Conspiracy," *New York Times*, October 18, 1977, 24, 77.

4. The Boston Fire Department's notoriously modest statistics show a drastic rise in arson fires, from 51 in 1969 to 693 in 1974. James P. Brady, "Arson, Fiscal Crisis, and Community Action: Dialectics of an Urban Crime and a Popular Response," *Crime & Delinquency* 28 (1982): 263.

5. Pete Stidman, "*Fenway News* Hires a New Editor," *Boston Courant*, June 30, 2007.

6. Ostrow, interview.

7. DOW was the chemical company that manufactured napalm. Faderman and Timmons, *Gay L.A.*, 172.

8. For more on Medicaid and Medicare fraud history, see Grace Budrys, *Planning for the Nation's Health: A Study of Twentieth-Century Developments in the United States* (New York: Greenwood Press, 1986); Engel, *Poor People's Medicine*; Mark Ross Daniels, *Medicaid Reform and the American States: Case Studies on the Politics of Managed Care* (Westport, Conn.: Auburn House, 1998); Laura Katz Olson, *The Politics of Medicaid* (New York: Columbia University Press); John W. Schilling, *Undercover: How I Went from Company Man to FBI Spy—and Exposed the Worst Healthcare Fraud in U.S. History* (New York: American Management Association, 2008).

9. William Hines, "Doctors Intensify Campaign Against Standards Review," *Chicago Sun-Times*, June 24, 1974, 38.

10. Engel, *Poor People's Medicine*; Olson, *The Politics of Medicaid*.

11. This is just one of many ways in which the straight state works to incentivize and privilege heterosexuality. For other examples, see Canaday, *The Straight State*.

12. On the national debate over single-payer or nationalized health care, see Engel, *Poor People's Medicine*; Karen Davis and Cathy Schoen, *Health and the War on Poverty: A Ten-Year Appraisal* (Washington, D.C.: Brookings Institution, 1978); Paul Starr, *The Social Transformation of American Medicine* (New York: Basic Books, 1982); John E. Murray, *Origins of American Health Insurance: A History of Industrial Sickness Funds* (New Haven, Conn.: Yale University Press, 2007); Beatrix Hoffman, *The Wages of Sickness: The Politics of Health Insurance in Progressive America* (Chapel Hill: University of North Carolina Press, 2001); Stevens, Rosenberg, and Burns, *History and Health Policy in the United States*; Quadagno, *One Nation, Uninsured*.

13. For more on the history of the American Medical Association, see Morris Fishbein, *A History of the American Medical Association, 1847 to 1947* (Philadelphia: Saunders, 1947); David J. Rothman, *Strangers at the Bedside: A History of How Law and Bioethics Transformed Medical Decision Making* (New Brunswick, N.J.: AldineTransaction, 2008).

14. Alberts, interview; Sally Deane, interview by author, August 2, 2007; Scondras, interview; Tobin and Brophy, interview.

15. Scondras, interview.

16. Fenway Community Health Center, "Opening New Doors . . ."; Vance, interview; Deane, interview; Rideout, interview; Alberts, interview; Scondras, interview.

17. Scondras, interview.

18. Fenway Community Health Center, "Opening New Doors . . ."

19. Discrepancies exist among those interviewed on just how long the debate over this lasted, ranging from days to nearly a year. A majority of sources claim that the debate took twenty-four hours spaced out over several days. Tobin and Brophy, interview; Rideout, interview; Scondras, interview.

20. Fenway Community Health Center, "Opening New Doors . . ."

21. Scondras, interview; Tobin and Brophy, interview; Fenway Community Health Center, "Opening New Doors . . ."

22. Tobin and Brophy, interview.

23. Fenway Community Health Center, "Opening New Doors . . ."

24. Alberts, interview.

25. Ibid.

26. Kilhefner, interview.

27. Ibid.

28. Governor's Commission on the Los Angeles Riots, "Violence in the City—an End or a Beginning?" (Los Angeles: The Governor's Commission, 1965). Also noteworthy is that the commission found that the lack of a nearby hospital and health services (the nearest emergency room was ten miles away at the University of Southern California) also contributed to the unrest in the community. On the Watts uprising, see Gerald Horne, *Fire This Time: The Watts Uprising and the 1960s* (Charlottesville: University Press of Virginia, 1995); Christopher B. Strain, *Pure Fire: Self-Defense as Activism in the Civil Rights Era* (Athens: University of Georgia Press, 2005); Hilliard, *The Black Panther Party*, 75. On the Black Panther Party, see Cleaver and Katsiaficas, *Liberation, Imagination, and the Black Panther Party*; Peniel E. Joseph, *The Black Power Movement: Rethinking the Civil Rights-Black Power Era* (New York: Routledge, 2006). The research of Alondra Nelson explores in depth the way that the Black Panther Party used health services both as a practical solution to community problems and as a political tool. See Nelson, *Body and Soul*.

29. On the fight for abortion rights, see Morgen, *Into Our Own Hands*; Linda Gordon, *The Moral Property of Women: A History of Birth Control Politics in America*, 3rd ed. (Urbana and Chicago: University of Illinois Press, 2002). On the politics of race and survival in reproductive rights activism among women of color, see Nelson, *Women of Color and the Reproductive Rights Movement*.

30. Alvin M. Josephy Jr., Joane Nagel, and Troy Johnson, eds., *Red Power: The American Indians' Fight for Freedom* (Lincoln: University of Nebraska Press, 1999); Troy Johnson, Joane Nagel, and Duane Champagne, eds., *American Indian Activism: Alcatraz to the Longest Walk* (Chicago: University of Illinois Press, 1997); Lawrence, "The Indian Health Service"; Bergman et al., "A Political History of the Indian Health Service."

31. Laura Pulido, *Black, Brown, Yellow, and Left: Radical Activism in Los Angeles* (Berkeley: University of California Press, 2006), 116; Randy Shaw, *Beyond the Fields: Cesar Chavez, the UFW, and the Struggle for Justice in the 21st Century* (Berkeley: University of California Press, 2008).

32. Scondras, interview; Renslow, interview; Ostrow, interview.

33. Renslow, interview; Deane, interview; Almena Brooks, Antonio Kropf, Ann Marchewka, and Ann O'Brien, "The Fenway Community Health Center: An Analysis of the Marketing Situation and a Marketing Plan," December 3, 1984, box 1, folder Marketing Plan 1984, Fenway Health Collection, #58, HPA.

34. Brooks, Kropf, Marchewka, O'Brien, "The Fenway Community Health Center."

35. Becky Thompson, "Multiracial Feminism: Recasting the Chronology of Second Wave Feminism," *Feminist Studies* 28, no. 2 (2002): 337–60; Nelson, *Women of Color and the Reproductive Rights Movement*; Morgen, *Into Our Own Hands*.

36. The field of obstetrics and gynecology often garnered the harshest criticism: "Rather than replace men with women and maintain the specialty, I propose we disband the specialty altogether and return the care of women to midwives and internists trained in primary care" (Helen Marieskind, "Restructuring Ob-Gyn," *Social Policy*, September/October 1975, 48). For more examples of critiques of mainstream medicine, see Helen Marieskind and Barbara Ehrenreich, "Toward Socialist Medicine: The Women's Health Movement," *Social Policy*, September/October 1975, 34–42; Barbara Seaman, "Pelvic Autonomy: Four Proposals," ibid., 43–47; Mary Howell, "A Women's Health School," ibid., 50–53; Barbara Rowland and Lawrence Schneiderman, "Women in Alternative Health Care: Their Influence on Traditional Medicine," *Journal of the American Medical Association* 241, no. 7 (1979): 719–21; Barbara Kaiser and Irwin Kaiser, "The Challenge of the Women's Movement to American Gynecology," *American Journal of Obstetrics and Gynecology* 120, no. 5 (1974): 652–65.

37. Gutierrez et al., *Undivided Rights*; Nelson, *Women of Color and the Reproductive Rights Movement*; Nelson, *Body and Soul*; Morgen, *Into Our Own Hands*; Amber Jamilla Musser, "From Our Body to Yourselves: The Boston Women's Health Book Collective and Changing Notions of Subjectivity, 1969–1973," *Women's Studies Quarterly* 35, no. 1/2 (2007): 93–109; Kathy Davis, *The Making of Our Bodies, Ourselves: How Feminism Travels Across Borders*, Next Wave (Durham, N.C.: Duke University Press, 2007); Nancy Ehrenreich, *The Reproductive Rights Reader* (New York: New York University Press, 2008).

38. "Carole Schmitz," *Gay Life*, July 21, 1978, 4–5.

39. This new feminist health movement took many forms, ranging from the Jane collective in Chicago, which organized and provided underground abortion services in the year before *Roe v. Wade* to the Boston Women's Health Book Collective to the New York City–based Redstockings. On these, see Laura Kaplan, *The Story of Jane: The Legendary Underground Feminist Abortion Service* (Chicago: University of Chicago Press, 1997); Musser, "From Our Body to Yourselves"; Davis, *The Making of Our Bodies, Ourselves*.

40. Mina Meyer, telephone interview by author, December 11, 2007.

41. Dick Nash, "Position Paper, 15 September," 1972, box 104-113, GCSCP.

42. Raphael, interview.

43. Ibid.

44. Meyer, interview.

45. Raphael, interview.

46. Ibid.

47. Meyer, interview.

48. Raphael, interview.

49. Los Angeles Gay Community Services Center, "Quarterly Report"; "Extended Pamphlet on the Gay Community Services Center," n.d., box 104-101, GCSCP.

50. "Van Ness Recovery House Second Annual Dinner Dance Program," 1975, box 247, folder 1, MKP.

51. "Articles of Incorporation," 1971, box 4, folder 2, MKP.

52. Meyer, interview.

53. Ibid.

54. Ibid.

55. Los Angeles Gay Community Services Center "Outreach: The Extended Family Newsletter, February," 1973, Gay and Lesbian Community Services Center Folder, MA; Meyer, interview; Los Angeles Regional Family Planning Council, "Family Planning Program Agreement Number 621," 1975, box 104-104, GCSCP.

56. Nearly every single interview with women from these clinics referenced sexism and pointed to examples ranging from gay men regularly asking women to take notes or make food during meetings to gay men's consistent lack of concern for programmatic equity, hostile takeovers of lesbian spaces, programs, or events, or reticence to include lesbian services.

57. Chichester, interview.

58. Ibid.

59. For more on the historic role of bars in gay culture, see Kennedy and Davis, *Boots of Leather, Slippers of Gold*; Howard, *Men Like That*; Chauncey, *Gay New York*; Stewart-Winter, *Queer Clout*; Brett Beemyn, *Creating a Place for Ourselves: Lesbian, Gay, and Bisexual Community Histories* (New York: Routledge, 1997).

60. Renslow, interview.

61. Chichester, interview.

62. Renslow, interview.

63. "I Want You for a Free VD Test," 1976, WLPC.

64. Chichester, interview.

65. Ibid.

66. Renslow, interview.

67. "Use of VD Clinic Run by Homosexuals Called Proof of Value," *Family Practice News* 7, no. 2 (1977): 1.

68. Kaplan, *The Story of Jane*; Nelson, *Women of Color and the Reproductive Rights Movement*; Nelson, *Body and Soul*; Morgen, *Into Our Own Hands*.

Chapter 3

1. Examples of this literature include Canaday, *The Straight State*; Regina Kunzel, *Criminal Intimacy: Prison and the Uneven History of Modern American Sexuality* (Chicago: University of Chicago Press, 2008); Luibhéid, *Entry Denied*; Somerville, *Queering the Color Line*; Dean Spade, *Normal Life: Administrative Violence, Critical Trans Politics, and the Limits of Law* (Durham, N.C.: Duke University Press, 2015); Self, *All in the Family*; Stewart-Winter, *Queer Clout*; Bell, *California Crucible*.

2. Most historians agree that the number of community health clinics receiving state funding hit a high-water mark in 1975. Engel, *Poor People's Medicine*, 135.

3. On the politics of community health clinics, see Lefkowitz, *Community Health Centers*; Alice Sardell, *The U.S. Experiment in Social Medicine: The Community Health Center Program, 1965–1986* (Pittsburgh: University of Pittsburgh Press, 1988); Engel, *Poor People's Medicine*; Craig E. Blohm, *The Great Society: America Fights the War on Poverty* (Farmington Hills, Mich.: Lucent Books, 2004); Stephen P. Strickland, *The History of Regional Medical Programs: The Life and Death of a Small Initiative of the Great Society* (Lanham, Md.: University Press of America, 2000).

4. Steve Metalitz, "Free Health Care in Chicago," *Chicago Reader*, June 16, 1972, 1; Lois Wille, "Homosexual Clergy Tells of His Bizarre Double Life," *Chicago Daily News*, June 21, 1966, 3–4.

5. Metalitz, "Free Health Care in Chicago."

6. Ostrow, interview.

7. Renslow, interview.

8. National Coalition of Gay STD Services, "National Coalition of Gay STD Services Fact Sheet," 1979, WLPC; Walter Lear, "GLPHWC Roots," 1990, WLPC.

9. "Letter to James Mongan, July 27," 1978, WLPC; "First Draft of a Proposal for a National Study Commission on the Health Concerns of Sexual Minorities," 1979, WLPC; Gay People in Medicine, "First National Gay Health Conference: The Health Closet," 1978, WLPC.

10. Howard Brown Memorial Clinic, "Howard Brown Memorial Clinic Quarterly Report," 1975, WLPC. This illustrates both the epidemic level of VD among the gay population and the gay community's aversion to going to the city-run clinics.

11. In Boston and Los Angeles, patients commonly used obviously fake or partial names without criticism or consequence. However, the Howard Brown clinic was the first to make it standard protocol to assign an anonymous "name" to each patient file that consisted of a combination of the patient's date of birth and mother's maiden name. Teller, interview; Kilhefner, interview; Mayer, interview.

12. Ostrow, interview.

13. Merv Walker, "The Clap Trap: A Venereal Catch 22," *Toronto Body Politic*, April, 1975, 15–16; D. G. Ostrow and N. L. Altman, "Sexually Transmitted Diseases and Homosexuality," *Sexually Transmitted Diseases* 10, no. 4 (1983): 208–15; Centers for Disease Control and Prevention, *Tracking the Hidden Epidemics*.

14. For more on federal regulation and community health clinics, see Engel, *Poor People's Medicine*; Lefkowitz, *Community Health Centers*; Sardell, *The U.S. Experiment in Social Medicine*; Dittmer, *The Good Doctors*; Stevens, *The Public-Private Health Care State*.

15. Ostrow, interview.

16. Howard Brown Memorial Clinic, "History of Howard Brown Memorial Clinic," 1981, box 7, David Ostrow Papers, GH.

17. Stevens, Rosenberg, and Burns, *History and Health Policy in the United States*; Irwin Miller, *American Health Care Blues: Blue Cross, HMOs, and Pragmatic Reform Since 1960* (New Brunswick, N.J.: Transaction Publishers, 1996); Lefkowitz, *Community*

Health Centers; Sardell, *The U.S. Experiment in Social Medicine*; Stevens, *The Public-Private Health Care State*; Gottschalk, *The Shadow Welfare State*.

18. Canaday, *The Straight State*.

19. Michel Foucault, *Discipline and Punish: The Birth of the Prison* (New York: Pantheon Books, 1977).

20. Jasbir K. Puar, *Terrorist Assemblages: Homonationalism in Queer Times* (Durham, N.C.: Duke University Press, 2007); Spade, *Normal Life*.

21. Alberts, interview.

22. Fenway Community Health Center, "Opening New Doors . . ."

23. "Every Week Events," *Gay Community News*, October 9, 1976, 15.

24. Tobin and Brophy, interview. These hospitals also regularly encouraged students and residents to volunteer their time at the Fenway clinic as state matching grants rewarded hospitals' service to underserved communities. David G. Smith and Judith D. Moore, *Medicaid Politics and Policy, 1965–2007* (New Brunswick, N.J.: Transaction Publishers, 2008); Engel, *Poor People's Medicine*; Mayer, interview; Alberts, interview.

25. Deane, interview.

26. Ibid.; Tobin and Brophy, interview.

27. Scondras, interview.

28. Ibid.

29. Ibid.

30. Tilo Schabert, *Boston Politics: The Creativity of Power* (New York: W. de Gruyter, 1989), 118–30; Tobin and Brophy, interview; Scondras, interview.

31. Fenway Community Health Center, "Opening New Doors . . ."

32. Ibid.

33. Deane, interview; Ron Vachon, "Letter to Walter Lear, August 16," 1978, WLPC.

34. Fenway Community Health Center, "Opening New Doors . . ."

35. John Graczak, "Investigation of Disease Will Begin in Co-Operative Effort," *Gay Community News*, October 28, 1978, 4.

36. Fenway Community Health Center, "Opening New Doors . . ."

37. Deane, interview.

38. Tobin and Brophy, interview.

39. Deane, interview.

40. Ibid.

41. Fenway Community Health Center, "Opening New Doors . . ."

42. Tobin and Brophy, interview.

43. Gay Feminist 11, "Shut Down Against Repression Leaflet," 1975, box 104-103, GCSCP.

44. "Women Speak out About GCSC," 1975, box 104-113, GCSCP.

45. Los Angeles Gay Community Services Center, "History and Objectives," 1976, box 104-114, GCSCP; "Explanation of Programs and Other Services," 1978, box 104-101, GCSCP.

46. Housing collective members, "'Gay Center' Shafts Gays!," 1973, Gay and Lesbian Community Services Center File, MA.

47. Ibid.

48. John F. McDonald, *Urban America: Growth, Crisis, and Rebirth* (Armonk, N.Y.: M. E. Sharpe, 2008); Stephen Strickland, *The History of Regional Medical Programs: The Life and Death of a Small Initiative of the Great Society* (Lanham, Md.: University Press of America, 2000); John A. Andrew, *Lyndon Johnson and the Great Society*, The American Ways Series (Chicago: I. R. Dee, 1998); Craig Blohm, *The Great Society: America Fights the War on Poverty* (Farmington Hills, Mich.: Lucent Books, 2004).

49. "Memorandum, 21 April," 1975, box 104-103, GCSCP; "Chronology of Recent Events at the Gay Community Services Center, 29 April," 1975, box 104-103, GCSCP; Honorable Board of Supervisors, "Contract with Gay Community Services Center, 28 November," 1975, box 104-103, GCSCP.

50. Meyer, interview.

51. Los Angeles Gay Community Services Center, "Outreach: The Extended Family Newsletter"; Meyer, interview; Los Angeles Regional Family Planning Council, "Family Planning Program Agreement."

52. This is one instance in which Canaday's notion of the "straight State" rings true in gay health activism in the 1970s, as the state regulations eclipsed the success of lesbian health care. Canaday, *The Straight State*.

53. Los Angeles Gay Community Services Center, "Commentary on the 1974 Financial Report."

54. "The Gay Community Services Center: Its History, Services & Problems," n.d., box 104-114, GCSCP, 5; "Minute Abstracted from the Minutes of the Meeting of the Board of Directors 30 April," 1975, box 104-102, GCSCP.

55. Sexual parity in services, leadership and management positions, and salaries was a continuous struggle and point of contention for many women involved with the center, as well as for many men who politically identified as feminists. In January 1975, just a few months before the crisis, thirty-three women workers met with members of the management team to discuss better ways of ensuring equal representation of the women workers in the center's decision making and to improve communication between management and women workers. Many men of the center wrote a statement of support for the women as they shared many of the same concerns. "Letter to the Board of Directors and Management Team of the Gay Community Services Center, 16 January," 1975, box 104-102, GCSCP; "Letter to the Board of Directors and Management Team, Regarding the Women's Letter to the Board and Management Team, 16 January," 1975, box 104-102, GCSCP.

56. "Meeting Minutes, 11 November," 1974, box 104-102, GCSCP.

57. Gay Feminist 11, "It's About Time . . . ," 1975, box 104-103, GCSCP.

58. Ibid.

59. Ibid.; Morris Kight, "Agenda Items Submitted by Morris Kight for Possible Inclusion, 25 April," 1975, box 104-103, GCSCP.

60. Gay Feminist 11, "It's About Time . . ."

61. Los Angeles Gay Community Services Center, "Memorandum, 21 April," 1975, box 104-103, GCSCP.

62. Ibid.

63. "Memorandum Demanding the Dismissal of Ken Bartley and Don Kilhefner," 1975, box 104-103, GCSCP.

64. "Chronology of Recent Events at the Gay Community Services Center, 29 April," 1975, box 104-103, GCSCP; Kight, "Agenda Items Submitted by Morris Kight."

65. Kight, "Agenda Items Submitted by Morris Kight."

66. "Gay Community Services Center Report, May," 1975, box 104-103, GCSCP, 2.

67. "Description of Each Dismissed Employee, Disseminated by the Gay Community Services Center," 1975, box 104-103, GCSCP.

68. Kight, "Agenda Items Submitted by Morris Kight."

69. Gay Feminist 11, "Serving the Gay and Lesbian Community: A Careful Look at the Board of Directors Leaflet," 1975, box 104-103, GCSCP.

70. "Why Boycott? Leaflet," 1975, box 104-103, GCSCP. It is worth noting that 5 of the Feminist 11 were actually men who politically identified as feminists.

71. "Letter to the Gay Feminist Sixteen," 1975, box 246, folder 2, MKP.

72. Teller, interview.

73. Gay Feminist 11, "Why Boycott?"; "Description of Each Dismissed Employee"; "Serving the Gay and Lesbian Community."

74. Faderman and Timmons, *Gay L.A.*, 204–5; Hobson, *Lavender and Red*.

75. Gay Feminist 11, "Why Boycott?"; Gay Feminist 11, "Shut Down Against Repression Leaflet," 1975, box 104-103, GCSCP; Gay Feminist 11, "Who's Who Leaflet," 1975, box 104-103, GCSCP.

76. Gay Community Services Center Board, "To the Gay Feminist Sixteen"; "Gay Community Services Center Report"; "Chronology of Recent Events."

77. "Women Speak out About GCSC," 1.

78. "Chronology of Recent Events"; Gay Community Services Center Board, "To the Gay Feminist Sixteen"; Los Angeles Gay Community Services Center, "Cover Letter for the Chronology of Recent Events at the Gay Community Services Center, 3 May," 1975, box 104-103, GCSCP; "Press Release: The Board of Directors of the Gay Community Services Center Recently Dismissed 11 Workers," 1975, box 104-103, GCSCP.

79. "Court Order to Show Cause Regarding Preliminary Injunction and Temporary Restraining Order, Case Number 124173, Superior Court of the State of California for the County of Los Angeles, Cordova et al. v. Gay Community Services Center," 1975, box 104-110, GCSCP.

80. "Settlement Agreement," 1978, box 104-112, GCSCP.

81. "Press Release: Recently Dismissed 11 Workers."

82. "Personnel Policies and Procedures Revised July–November," 1977, box 251, folder 6, MKP; "General Policies and Procedures," 1978, box 104-101, GCSCP.

83. "Settlement Agreement."

84. "Introduction and Historical Perspective," 1–12; "Preliminary Financial Statements"; "History and Objectives."

85. "Introduction and Historical Perspective," 14.

86. "Fact Sheet."

87. Stephen Schulte, "Memorandum, HUD Grant for Purchase of Building, 26 June," 1980, box 104-102, GCSCP; Morris Kight, "Letter to Sheldon Andelson, Regarding Gay Communtiy Services Center, Ceta, Title VI Funding, 5 October," 1977, box 104-112, GCSCP; Los Angeles County, "The Requirements for Eligibility for CETA Jobs," 1977, box 104-101, GCSCP; Faderman and Timmons, *Gay L.A.*, 208.

88. Tobin and Brophy, interview.

Chapter 4

1. Ostrow, interview.

2. Ibid.

3. John Elmer, "Malpractice Bill OKd with Arbitration Clause," *Chicago Tribune*, June 22, 1976, 2.

4. "Chicago's Lincoln Park Lagooners Present Winter Carnival Benefit 1976," *Gay Life*, March 5, 1976, 17.

5. Ostrow, interview.

6. "Chicago's Lincoln Park Lagooners."

7. Ostrow, interview.

8. Ibid.; Tom Peters, "Clinic Splits from Gay Horizons," *Gay Life*, September 3, 1976, 1.

9. Tom Peters, "Coalition Ponders Community Finances," *Gay Life*, July 23, 1976, 2; Ostrow, interview.

10. Peters, "Coalition Ponders Community Finances."

11. Peters, "Clinic Splits from Gay Horizons."

12. Dale Shaskey, "Letter to Mr. Allen Kelson, September 8," 1976, WLPC.

13. "Description of Howard Brown Memorial Clinic Research Site," 1978, box 3, David Ostrow Papers, GH.

14. "Chicago Gay Health Project Holds Annual Dinner on December 8th," *Gay Life*, October 30, 1977, 2; "Minutes for the Board of Directors Meeting, April 8," 1978, box 5, David Ostrow Papers, GH; "Board Meeting Minutes, January 2," 1978, box 5, David Ostrow Papers, GH; "Clinic Needs More Space," *Gay Life*, March 31, 1978, 2; "Howard Brown Clinic Month Set," *Gay Life*, August 17, 1979, 2; "Brief History of the Brown Clinic," *Gay Life*, September 7, 1979, 3.

15. Charlie Mehler, "The Howard Brown Clinic: Its History and Range of Services," *Gay Life*, June 22, 1979, 2; "VD Van Cruises Again: Free Disease Screening Offered," *Gay Life*, August 31, 1979, 8; "New VD Clinic in Gay Ghetto? VD Bus Patronage Exceeds Goal," *Chicago Gay Crusader* 23 (1975): 1, 8; Howard Brown Memorial Clinic, "Howard Brown Memorial Clinic Quarterly Report," 1975, WLPC.

16. "Use of VD Clinic Run by Homosexuals Called Proof of Value," *Family Practice News* 7, no. 2 (1977): 1.

17. The extensive "services listing" in *Gay Community News* throughout the 1970s occasionally included gay health clinic information for a clinic in Vermont and another in western Massachusetts, but these listings were very inconsistent. Additionally, mental health services, including rap sessions, were plentiful for both gays and lesbians in Boston, yet physical health services within the city, and generally in the region, were limited to those offered by the Fenway clinic. Meanwhile, the Gay Health Collective grew to two nights per week starting in late 1976. "Every Week Events," *Gay Community News*, October 9, 1976, 15; John Graczak, "Investigation of Disease Will Begin in Co-Operative Effort," *Gay Community News*, October 28, 1978, 4.

18. Deane, interview.

19. Alberts, interview.

20. The emergence of gay health services in the absence of gay health activism was not unique to the Fenway clinic, though the Boston clinic appears to be the only one that was not a public health clinic that evolved this way. Public health clinics in San Francisco, New York City, Denver, and Seattle went to great lengths to attract and cater to a gay clientele, gaining reputations locally and nationally as gay health clinics, even though they were actually public health clinics intended for the general population. Michael Brown and Larry Knopp, "The Birth of the (Gay) Clinic," *Health & Place* 28 (2014): 99–108.

21. See Bruce Schulman, *The Seventies: The Great Shift in American Culture, Society, and Politics* (New York: Free Press, 2001); Edward D. Berkowitz, *Something Happened: A Political and Cultural Overview of the Seventies* (New York: Columbia University Press, 2006); Stephanie A. Slocum-Schaffer, *America in the Seventies* (Syracuse, N.Y.: Syracuse University Press, 2003); Sam Binkley, *Getting Loose: Lifestyle Consumption in the 1970s* (Durham, N.C.: Duke University Press, 2007); David Frum, *How We Got Here: The 70's, the Decade That Brought You Modern Life (for Better or Worse)* (New York: Basic Books, 2000); Andreas Killen, *1973 Nervous Breakdown: Watergate, Warhol, and the Birth of Post-Sixties America* (New York: Bloomsbury; Distributed to the trade by Holtzbrinck, 2006).

22. "The Cambridge Women's Center Newsletter, September/October," 1980, box 94, folder 5, SL.

23. The incidence of highly resistant strains of VD grew steadily in the waning years of the decade, resulting in new clients and more visits from some existing clients. While at the time doctors were unsure of the spike in these cases, we now know they were the early stages of what would become the AIDS crisis. Alberts, interview.

24. Deane, interview.

25. Tom Reeves, "Boston's Boring Whiteness," *Gay Community News*, November 11, 1978, 4.

26. "Violence Against Gays Continues in Boston," *Gay Community News*, October 7, 1978, 1.

27. "Fenway Mugging," *Gay Community News*, July 12, 1973, 1; "Boston Man Paralyzed in Shooting," *Gay Community News*, October 28, 1978, 1.

28. Deane, interview.

29. Ibid.; Fenway Community Health Center, "Opening New Doors . . ."

30. Tobin and Brophy, interview. The AIDS crisis that appeared in Boston in the fall of 1981 seems to have either eclipsed or undercut outreach efforts specifically for racial minorities and low-income people not infected or affected by the AIDS crisis itself. The clinic struggled to meet the needs of a clientele that was both growing and facing much more extreme health issues than the clinic had previously managed. However, by the middle of the decade, the clinic implemented outreach programs for these communities, many of which continue today.

31. Alberts, interview.

32. Feuer, interview by author, January 30, 2014.

33. Deane, interview; Susan Robinson, interview by author, August 1, 2007.

34. Catherine Batza, "From Sperm Runners to Sperm Banks: Lesbians, Assisted Conception, and the Fertility Industry, 1971–1983," *Journal of Women's History* 28, no. 2 (Summer 2016): 82–102.

35. Los Angeles Gay Community Services Center, "'Don't Give Him Anything But Love' Poster," n.d., box 104-103, GCSCP; "Gay Love Needs Care Poster," 1972, box 104-101, GCSCP; "A Shot in the Ass Gala Benefit Program," 1975, Gay and Lesbian Community Services Center File, MA.

36. "User Profile of GCSC Clinic," n.d., box 254, folder 4, MKP; David Ostrow and Dale Shaskey, "The Experience of the Howard Brown Memorial Clinic of Chicago with Sexually Transmitted Diseases," *Sexually Transmitted Diseases* 4, no. 2 (1977): 53–55; Donald Barrett, William Darrow, Karla Jay, and Allen Young, "The Gay Report on Sexually Transmitted Diseases," *American Journal of Public Health* 71, no. 9 (1981): 1004–11; Karla Jay and Allen Young, *The Gay Report: Lesbian and Gay Men Speak Out About Sexual Experiences and Lifestyles* (New York: Summit Books, 1979).

37. Meyer, interview.

38. Los Angeles Gay Community Services Center, "Outreach: The Extended Family Newsletter."

39. Ostrow and Shaskey, "The Experience of the Howard Brown Memorial Clinic"; Harrison, "Straight Talk from a Gay Doctor," 34–36; Tom Maurer, "Health Care and the Gay Community," *Postgraduate Medicine* 58, no. 1 (1975): 127–30; "Gays Win Recognition at A.P.H.A Convention," *Gay Health Reports: Newsletter of Gay Public Health Workers, A Caucus of the A.P.H.A.* 1, no. 1 (1976): 1–2, 4; Henry Kazal et al., "The Gay Bowel Syndrome: Clinico-Pathologic Correlation in 260 Cases," *Annals of Clinical and Laboratory Science* 6, no. 2 (1976): 184–92; Walter Lear, "Venereal Disease and Gay Men: Opening Remarks," *Sexually Transmitted Diseases* 4, no. 2 (1977): 49; Golin, "MDs Assess Problems in Treating Gays"; Dorothy Riddle, "Relating to Children: Gays as Role Models," *Journal of Social Issues* 34, no. 3 (1978): 38–58; "Use of VD Clinic Run by Homosexuals"; Yehudi Felman and John Morrison, "Examining the Homosexual Male for Sexually Transmitted Diseases," *Journal of the American Medical Association* 238, no. 19 (1977): 2046–47; Leon Speroff, "The Clinician and the Homosexual Patient," *Contemporary OB/*

GYN 14 (1979): 92–107; Jay and Young, *The Gay Report*; Ostrow and Shaskey, "The Experience of the Howard Brown Memorial Clinic."

40. Mehler, "The Howard Brown Clinic."

41. Harrison, "Straight Talk from a Gay Doctor"; Robert Fass, "Sexual Transmission of Viral Hepatitis?," *Journal of the American Medical Association* 230, no. 6 (1974): 861–62; Chris Coste, "Gay Doctors Edging out of the Closet," *New Physician*, 1974, 30–33; Walter Merten and Sylvia Nothman, "Neighborhood Health Center Experience: Implications for Project Grants," *American Journal of Public Health* 65 (1975): 248; Maurer, "Health Care and the Gay Community"; Wolf Szumuness et al., "On the Role of Sexual Behavoir in the Spread of Hepatitis B Infection," *Annals of Internal Medicine* 83 (1975): 489–95; Kazal et al., "The Gay Bowel Syndrome"; Ostrow and Shaskey, "The Experience of the Howard Brown Memorial Clinic"; Lear, "Venereal Disease and Gay Men"; K. S. Lim et al., "Role of Sexual and Non-Sexual Practices in the Transmission of Hepatitis B," *British Journal of Venereal Diseases* 53 (1977): 190–92; Felman and Morrison, "Examining the Homosexual Male"; "Use of VD Clinic Run by Homosexuals"; Golin, "MDs Assess Problems in Treating Gays"; Yehudi Felman and James Nikitas, "Sexually Transmitted Enteric Pathogens in New York City," *New York State Journal of Medicine*, 1979, 1412–13; Felman and Nikitas, "Epidemiologic Approach to Control of Sexually Transmitted Disease," ibid., 745–46; Speroff, "The Clinician and the Homosexual Patient"; Daniel William, "Sexually Transmitted Diseases in Gay Men: An Insider's View," *Sexually Transmitted Diseases* 6, no. 4 (1979): 278–80; William Janda et al., "Prevalence and Site-Pathogen Studies of Neisseria Meningitidis and N Gonorrhoeae in Homosexual Men," *Journal of the American Medical Association* 244, no. 18 (1980): 2060–64; Yehudi Felman, "Homosexual Hazards," *Practitioner* 224 (1980): 1151–56; David Ostrow et al., "Epidemiology of Gonorrhea Infections in Gay Men," *Journal of Homosexuality* 5, no. 3 (1980): 285–89; Robert Bolan, "Nonspecific Proctitis," ibid., 299–305; Alfred Baker, "Chronic Type B Hepatitis in Gay Men: Experience with Patients Referred from the Howard Brown Memorial Clinic to the University of Chicago," ibid., 311–51; Marshall Schreeder et al., "Epidemiology of Hepatitis B Infection in Gay Men," ibid., 307–10; William M. Janda, "Sexually-Transmitted Diseases in Homosexual Men," *Clinical Microbiology Newsletter* 3, no. 3 (1981): 15–17; Darrow et al., "The Gay Report on Sexually Transmitted Diseases," 1004–11; Daniel William, "The Sexual Transmission of Parasitic Infections in Gay Men," *Journal of Homosexuality* 5, no. 3 (1980): 291–93.

42. David Ostrow, "Letter from David Ostrow to Mark Bolan August 21," 1979, box 0, David Ostrow Papers, GH; "Letter to Walter Lear," 1976, WLPC; "Follow-Up Letter for August HBMC Board Meeting," 1980, box 8, Board Meetings folder, David Ostrow Papers, GH; Walter Lear, "Walter Lear to Friends," 1975, WLPC; "Letter to Hugo Muriel, January 28," 1982, box 5, Correspondence folder, David Ostrow Papers, GH; "Letter to Chuck Renslow, January 5," 1981, box 5, Board Meeting Minutes folder, Howard Brown Memorial Clinic Papers, GH; Shaskey, "Letter to Mr. Allen Kelson,"; "Letter to David Ostrow, May 28," 1981, box 7, David Ostrow Papers, GH.

43. American Psychological Association, "Memo Regarding the Status of Homosexuality

as a Mental Disorder," 1973, WLPC; "22,000 Psychiatrists Vote on Homosexuality," *Gay Community News*, February 16, 1974, 1; American Psychological Association, "Press Release," 1975, WLPC; Jack Drescher and Joseph P. Merlino, *American Psychiatry and Homosexuality: An Oral History* (New York: Harrington Park Press, 2007). Another important exception here is that in a handful of British and Australian medical journals researchers were beginning to hypothesize the relationship between homosexuals and the high incidence of hepatitis B. See Szumuness et al., "On the Role of Sexual Behavoir"; Fass, "Sexual Transmission of Viral Hepatitis?"; Lim et al., "Role of Sexual and Non-Sexual Practices."

44. For examples of the more prominent and influential articles, see Harrison, "Straight Talk from a Gay Doctor"; Maurer, "Health Care and the Gay Community"; Kazal et al., "The Gay Bowel Syndrome"; Felman and Morrison, "Examining the Homosexual Male"; Lear, "Venereal Disease and Gay Men"; Ostrow and Shaskey, "The Experience of the Howard Brown Memorial Clinic of Chicago with Sexually Transmitted Diseases"; Golin, "MDs Assess Problems in Treating Gays"; Felman and Nikitas, "Epidemiologic Approach"; Speroff, "The Clinician and the Homosexual Patient"; William, "Sexually Transmitted Diseases in Gay Men"; Baker, "Chronic Type B Hepatitis in Gay Men."

45. "Clinic Needs More Space"; "Description of Howard Brown Memorial Clinic Research Site."

46. "Description of Howard Brown Memorial Clinic Research Site."

47. David Ostrow and Dale Shaskey, "The VD Epidemiological Experience of the Howard Brown Memorial Clinic of Chicago"; "City Recognizes Howard Brown Clinic," *Gay Life*, September 14, 1979, 3; "Meeting of the Board of Directors of the Clinic, May 25," 1975, box 5, Board Meeting Minutes folder, David Ostrow Papers, GH; "New VD Clinic in Gay Ghetto?"; "Minutes of the Fifth Board Meeting of the Howard Brown Memorial Clinic," 1977, box 8, 1977 folder, Howard Brown Memorial Clinic Papers, GH; "Minutes for the Board of Directors Meeting"; "Board Meeting Minutes"; "Description of Howard Brown Memorial Clinic Research Site."

48. David Ostrow, "Research Director's Report, January 12," 1981, box 8, Howard Brown Memorial Clinic Papers, GH; "Confidential Notes from Meeting with Gary Coslett from Abbott Laboratories, February 8," 1982, box 8, Howard Brown Memorial Clinic Papers, GH; "History of Howard Brown," 1983, box 7, David Ostrow Papers, GH; "Description of Howard Brown Memorial Clinic Research Site"; David Ostrow, "An Epidemiological Study of Venereal Disease Among Male Homosexuals: A Research Proposal," 1975, box 5, STD Archives folder, David Ostrow Papers, GH.

49. Ostrow, interview.

50. Ibid.; Szumuness et al., "On the Role of Sexual Behavoir"; Fass, "Sexual Transmission of Viral Hepatitis?"

51. David Ostrow, "Letter to Dr. Pierce Gardner," 1976, David Ostrow Papers, GH.

52. William W. Darrow and the Hepatitis Collaborative Working Group, "Hepatitis B Virus in Gay Men: Pretest Procedures and Results for San Francisco and Chicago (HBMC)," 1977, David Ostrow Papers, GH.

53. The research actually resulted in numerous articles over the next couple of years. Darrow, Barrett, Jay, and Young, "The Gay Report on STDs"; Darrow et al., "The Gay Report on Sexually Transmitted Diseases"; Janda, "Sexually-Transmitted Diseases in Homosexual Men"

54. Howard Brown Memorial Clinic, "Staff Update, Volume 1, Number 2," 1978, David Ostrow Papers, GH.

55. Ostrow, interview.

56. Centers for Disease Control, Venereal Disease Control Division, "Operational Manual for Hepatitis B Study," 1977, David Ostrow Papers, GH; City of Chicago Department of Health, "City of Chicago Professional Service Contract,"1978, David Ostrow Papers, GH; Cedric Chernick, "Professional Service Contract Between the University of Chicago and Howard Brown Memorial Clinic," 1978, David Ostrow Papers, GH; Howard Brown Memorial Clinic, "Organizational Flow Chart of the Hepatitis B Study," 1978, David Ostrow Papers, GH.

57. David Bennett, Merino Hernando, Franklyn Judson, and Thomas Schaffnitt, "Screening for Gonorrhea and Syphilis in the Gay Bath Houses: A Comparative Study of Programs in Denver, Colorado, and Los Angeles, California" (paper presented at the 105th Annual Meeting of the American Public Health Association, Washington, D.C., November 3, 1977); "National Coalition of Gay STD Services Fact Sheet," 1979, WLPC; David Ostrow, "Letter to Mark Behar, December 29," 1980, box 8, David Ostrow Papers, GH; Ostrow, "Follow-Up Letter."

58. "Press Release and Article for the Hepatitis Vaccine Study," 1979, box 104-101, GCSCP.

59. Howard Brown Memorial Clinic, "You May Be Able to Prevent Hepatitis," n.d., WLPC.

60. Jeff Lyon, "Hepatitis May Have Found Its Match on Halsted Street," *Chicago Tribune*, January 21, 1981, 1, 4; Howard Brown Memorial Clinic, "You May Be Able to Prevent Hepatitis"; "Press Release for the Hepatitis Vaccine Study"; Stephen Kulieke, "Chicago's Howard Brown Clinic Takes Aim at Hepatitis," *Advocate* 240 (1982); "Press Release Regarding the Hepatitis B Vaccine Trials, March 26," 1979, WLPC; "City Recognizes Howard Brown Clinic"; "Hep B Vaccine Patient Information Sheet," 1982, WLPC.

61. "Press Release for the Hepatitis Vaccine Study."

62. Ibid.

63. Paul A. Offit, *Vaccinated: One Man's Quest to Defeat the World's Deadliest Diseases* (New York: Collins, 2007); Baruch S. Blumberg, *Hepatitis B: The Hunt for a Killer Virus* (Princeton, N.J.: Princeton University Press, 2002).

64. Venereal Disease Control Division, "Operational Manual."

65. Ostrow, interview; Lyon, "Hepatitis May Have Found Its Match"; Kulieke, "Chicago's Howard Brown Clinic Takes Aim"; "Press Release for the Hepatitis Vaccine Study."

66. "Hep B Vaccine Patient Information Sheet."

67. Ibid.; Chris Heim, "Hepatitis Vaccine Ready, but Cost High," *Gay Life*, July 23, 1982, 1, 9; Thomas J. Leonard, "Hepatitis Program Running Smoothly," *Gay Life*, August

2, 1980, 7, 18; "'Safe' Hepatitis Vaccine Now Available at Howard Brown Clinic," *Gay Life*, November 7, 1980, 11; Tom Myles, "Hepatitis Vaccine Test Program in the Works," *Gay Life*, January 18, 1980, 1, 5, 20; "Hepatitis B Vaccine Program Begins at HBMC," *Gay Life*, March 21, 1980, 3.

68. Heim, "Hepatitis Vaccine Ready"; Leonard, "Hepatitis Program Running Smoothly"; "'Safe' Hepatitis Vaccine Now Available at Howard Brown Clinic"; Myles, "Hepatitis Vaccine Test Program in the Works"; "Hepatitis B Vaccine Program Begins at HBMC."

69. "Confidential Notes from Meeting."

70. Lawrence M. Fisher, "Biotechnology Spotlight Now Shines on Chiron," *New York Times,* October 13, 1986.

71. Ostrow, interview. Though the production process of the plasma-based hepatitis B vaccine effectively killed the HIV virus, the perceived risk, combined with the availability of a cheaper and yeast-based vaccine, proved the death knell for the initial vaccine.

72. Felman and Morrison, "Examining the Homosexual Male"; James Spada, *The Spada Report: The Newest Survey of Gay Male Sexuality* (New York: New American Library, 1979).

73. Felman and Morrison, "Examining the Homosexual Male"; R. D. Fenwick, *The Advocate Guide to Gay Health* (New York: Dutton, 1978); "Chicago Gay Health Project Celebrates Anniversary," *Gay Life*, January 12, 1979, 18; "VD Control: A Moral and Legal Dilemma for Homosexuals," *Homosexual Information Center Newsletter*, April 1974, 1–4.

Chapter 5

1. Alberts, interview.

2. National Coalition of Gay STD Services, "NCGSTDS Member Services," *Official Newsletter of the National Coalition of Gay STD Services* 3, no. 2 (1981).

3. The Gay Community Services VD Clinic of Tucson actually opted to sever ties with state and federal funding just months before the start of the AIDS crisis because threats of funding cuts placed greater strain on the staff than simply operating on their own with limited hours of operations and volunteer staff. "Tucson's Gay VD Clinic Reopens," *Official Newsletter of the National Coalition of Gay STD Services* 2, no. 1 (1980).

4. "Clinic Evaluations," *Official Newsletter of the National Coalition of Gay STD Services* 2, no. 1 (1980).

5. "NCGSTDS Member Services."

6. "Report on the Bath-House Project," 1975, box 104-104, GCSCP; Vachon, "Letter to Walter Lear, August 16."

7. Felman, "Homosexual Hazards"; Felman and Nikitas, "Epidemiologic Approach"; Yehudi and James Nikitas Felman, "Sexually Transmitted Enteric Pathogens in New York City"; Felman and Morrison, "Examining the Homosexual Male"; Myles, "Hepatitis Vaccine Test Program in the Works."

8. Bennett et al., "Screening for Gonorrhea and Syphilis in the Gay Bath Houses";

Ostrow, "Research Director's Report"; Howard Brown Memorial Clinic, "Organizational Flow Chart"; "Gay Health Project Information Sheet," 1975, WLPC; Denver Department of Health and Hospitals, "V.D. Facts—Take One," 1976, WLPC.

9. "Chicago Gay Health Project Celebrates Anniversary"; "Midwest Baths Guide," *Gay Life*, March 2, 1979, 11, 13; National Coalition of Gay STD Services, "Announcements," *Official Newsletter of the National Coalition of Gay STD Services* 1, no. 2 (1979).

10. Marie Kuda and Michael Bergeron, "Reader's Guide to Gay Life," *Chicago Reader*, September 26, 1975, 42–43, 47.

11. Walter Lear, "Walter Lear Resume," 2006, WLPC.

12. Lear later wrote, "I was shocked out of my closeted life-style by the death of my close friend Howard J. Brown in February 1975" (Lear, "GLPHWC Roots").

13. Lear, "GLPHWC Roots."

14. Ibid.

15. "Walter Lear to Friends"; "Gays Win Recognition."

16. Bennett et al., "Screening for Gonorrhea and Syphilis in the Gay Bath Houses"; Vachon, "Letter to Walter Lear, August 16."

17. "Gay Public Health Workers Steering Committee Meeting Agenda and Minutes, December 17–18," 1977, WLPC; "Gay Public Health Workers Steering Committee Meeting Minutes, February 25–26," 1978, WLPC; "Gay Public Health Workers Steering Committee Meeting Minutes, April 15," 1978, WLPC; "Gay Public Health Workers Meeting Minutes, July 8–9," 1978, WLPC.

18. As much of lesbian health activism in this period intentionally occurred outside the medical mainstream and without medical professionals, whether in feminist self-help clinics or in other venues connected to the New Age movement, lesbian-specific health was not one of the major issues addressed in either the APHA's Gay Public Health Workers Caucus or the National Gay Health Coalition.

19. Gay People in Medicine, "First National Gay Health Conference."

20. Gay People in Medicine, "Gay People in Medicine Application Form," n.d., WLPC.

21. Ostrow, "Letter to Mark Behar, December 29"; Lyon, "Hepatitis May Have Found Its Match."

22. Robert A. Becker to David Ostrow, June 3, 1983, letter, box 1, David Ostrow Papers, GH.

23. "Third National Lesbian and Gay Health Conference Program of Events," 1980, WLPC.

24. New York University Post-Graduate Medical School, "The 1981 International Symposium on Viral Hepatitis, Conference Program," 1981, box 1, David Ostrow Papers, GH.

25. "National Coalition of Gay STD Services Fact Sheet."

26. Paul J. Wiesner, "Response," *Official Newsletter of the National Coalition of Gay STD Services* 1, no. 4 (1980); "Keynote Announcement," *Official Newsletter of the National Coalition of Gay STD Services* 1, no. 5 (1980).

27. David Ostrow, *AIDS Federal Funding Testimony, Before the House Labor, Health and Human Services, and Education Appropriations Subcommittee*, May 12, 1983.

28. "CDC Sponsored Meeting," *Official Newsletter of the National Coalition of Gay STD Services* 2, no. 2 (1980): 8.

29. Robert Bolan, "Guidelines and Recommendations for Healthful Gay Sexual Activity," supplement to the *Official Newsletter of the National Coalition of Gay STD Services* 3, no. 1 (1981).

30. "Walter Lear and Others Arrested at White House for Non-Violent Protest," *Official Newsletter of the National Coalition of Gay STD Services* 3, no. 1 (1981): 1.

31. Omnibus Budget Reconciliation Act of 1981, H.R. 3982, 97th Cong. (1981), https://www.govtrack.us/congress/bills/97/hr3982, accessed January 14, 2016.

32. Walter Lear, *Testimony at the House Subcommittee on Health*, April 3, 1981, https://profiles.nlm.nih.gov/ps/access/QQBCCD.pdf, accessed January 19, 2016.

33. Canaday, *The Straight State*.

34. "CDC Sponsored Gay STD Research Priorities Meeting Postponed Indefinitely," *Official Newsletter of the National Coalition of Gay STD Services* 3, no. 1 (1981): 2.

35. Ibid.

36. Centers for Disease Control, "Spectinomycin-Resistant Penicillinase-Producing Neisseria gonorrhoeae—California." *MMWR: Morbidity and Mortality Weekly Report* 30, no. 19 (1981): 221–22.

37. A. E. Friedman-Kien, L. Laubenstein, M. Marmor, K. Hymes, J. Green, A. Ragaz, J. Gottleib, F. Muggia, R. Demopoulos, and M. Weintraub, "Kaposis sarcoma and Pneumocystis pneumonia Among Homosexual Men—New York City and California," *MMWR: Morbidity and Mortality Weekly Report* 30, no. 25 (1981): 305–8.

38. Thomas Nylund, "News from Los Angeles," *Official Newsletter of the National Coalition of Gay STD Services* 3, no. 1 (1981): 12.

39. "STD Health Bulletin," *Official Newsletter of the National Coalition of Gay STD Services* 3, no. 1 (1981): 1.

40. Ostrow, *AIDS Federal Funding Testimony*.

41. Anita Diamant, "The Good Fight," *Boston Globe Magazine*, August 27, 1989, 59.

42. Ibid., 17, 59–68.

43. Feuer, interview.

44. Diamant, "The Good Fight," 17, 59–68.

45. Alberts, interview; Mayer, interview.

46. Initially, doctors called the disease GRID (Gay Related Immune Deficiency) or AID (Acquired Immune Deficiency) until formally agreeing on AIDS at one such conference in Washington, D.C., in 1982. Though short-lived, GRID helped set the narrative that the new disease infected only gay men, creating unnecessary political, public relations, and public health hurdles that still linger today. National Gay Task Force, National Gay Health Coalition, National Gay Health Education Foundation, *Program for AID FORUM*, Dallas Leadership Conference, August 13–15 1982, box 7, folder "Gay Men's Health Crisis G.M.H.C.," Lawrence Mass Papers, New York Public Library, New York.

47. "STD Health Bulletin," 1.

48. Renslow, interview.

49. Ostrow, interview. Glory hole rooms are rooms in which holes have been cut into the wall or partition for penises. A person would insert the penis into the hole from one side of the wall and an often-anonymous sexual partner would fellate them from the other side of the wall. In bathhouses, these rooms were designed at different floor heights so that both partners would be standing up and so that anal sex through the glory hole was impossible. Thus, replacing private rooms where patrons could have higher-risk anal sex with glory hole rooms that only allowed for blow jobs minimized the risk of HIV transmission significantly.

50. Ostrow, interview.

51. Ostrow, *AIDS Federal Funding Testimony*.

52. Ron Vachon and Dan Pfeffer, "National Gay Health Coalition: Networking for Social Change and Political Action," *Official Newsletter of the National Coalition of Gay STD Services* 3, no. 3.

53. Ostrow, interview.

54. "Mission and History," Fenway Health, http://fenwayhealth.org/about/history/, accessed January 19, 2016.

55. "MACS," StatEpi Coordinating Center, Department of Epidemiology, Johns Hopkins School of Hygiene and Public Health, https://statepi.jhsph.edu/macs/macs.html, accessed January 20, 2016.

Epilogue

1. Scott Colinico, "When Aids Was Funny," *Vanity Fair*, November 2015, http://www.vanityfair.com/news/2015/11/reagan-administration-response-to-aids-crisis2015.

2. Carroll, *Mobilizing New York*; Brier, *Infectious Ideas*; Cindy Patton, *Inventing AIDS* (New York: Routledge, 1990); Patton, *Sex and Germs: The Politics of AIDS* (Boston: South End Press, 1985); Cohen, *The Boundaries of Blackness*; Deborah Gould, *Moving Politics: Emotion and ACT UP's Fight Against AIDS,* (Chicago: University of Chicago Press, 2009); Steven Epstein, *Impure Science: AIDS, Activism, and the Politics of Knowledge* (Los Angeles: University of California Press, 1996); Douglas Crimp, *Melancholia and Moralism: Essays on AIDS and Queer Politics* (Boston: MIT Press, 2004); Victoria Harden, *AIDS at 30: A History* (Dulles, Va.: Potomac Books, 2012); Paula Treichler, *How to Have Theory in an Epidemic* (Durham, N.C.: Duke University Press, 1999); Larry Kramer, *Reports from the Holocaust: The Making of an AIDS Activist* (New York: St. Martin's Press, 1989); Jonathan Engel, *The Epidemic: A Global History of AIDS* (Washington, D.C.: Smithsonian Press, 2006); Roger Hallas, *Reframing Bodies: AIDS, Bearing Witness, and the Queer Moving Image* (Durham, N.C.: Duke University Press, 2009); Courtney Bender, *Heaven's Kitchen: Living Religion at God's Love We Deliver* (Chicago: University of Chicago Press, 2003); Sarah Schulman, *Stage Struck: Theater, AIDS, and the Marketing of Gay America* (Durham, N.C.: Duke University Press, 1998).

3. This is not to say that AIDS activism before ACT UP has been entirely overlooked by historians. Jennifer Brier offers a great example of research that reaches beyond the

confines of ACT UP, while also engaging with it in important ways. Brier, *Infectious Ideas*; Cohen, *The Boundaries of Blackness*.

4. Lisa Duggan, *The Twilight of Equality? Neoliberalism, Cultural Politics, and the Attack on Democracy* (Boston: Beacon Press, 2003), 179.

5. David L. Eng, *The Feeling of Kinship: Queer Liberalism and the Racialization of Intimacy* (Durham, N.C.: Duke University Press, 2010); Puar, *Terrorist Assemblages*; Duggan, *The Twilight of Equality?*; Spade, *Normal Life*.

6. Sari L. Reisner et al., "'Counting' Transgender and Gender-Nonconforming Adults in Health Research: Recommendatioins from the Gender Identity in US Surveillance Group," *Transgender Studies Quarterly* 2, no. 1 (2015); Harper Jean Tobin, Raffi Freedman-Gurspan, and Lisa Mottet, "A Blueprint for Equality: A Federal Agenda for Transgender People" (Washington, D.C.: National Center for Transgender Equality, 2015).

INDEX

Page numbers in italics refer to figures.

ACKNOWLEDGMENTS

I've been dreaming of writing these pages for over a decade, and yet I feel certain that they will fail to fully convey my deep appreciation and gratitude to all of those who have, in ways both big and small, nurtured this project from the earliest inklings to the full-fledged book. There are four people without whom I cannot imagine this book ever being written or published: John D'Emilio, Jennie Brier, Margot Canaday, and Bob Lockhart. I feel fortunate to have John D'Emilio as a mentor, both in graduate school and beyond. He has modeled the highest caliber of scholarship, demonstrated the true art of teaching, sparked the creation of a new field of academic inquiry that inspires activism and critical engagement with the world and its past, and possesses the best giggle in all the universe. His prodigious skills as a teacher and writer are dwarfed only by his kindness and humanity. Jennifer Brier has provided me with a template for my career as well as an example for how I hope to engage with the world as a scholar and a human. Her generosity, wit, passion, and ideas are both inspiring and, well, infectious. Margot Canaday's brilliance, encouragement, and insight have shaped this book through the prodding questions, thoughtful comments, and careful shepherding of a skilled series editor. She has found the perfect balance between allowing me to find my own way and supplying useful navigation as needed or requested. I appreciate her time and dedication to rigorous scholarship, mentoring junior scholars, and seeing my project become its best possible version of itself. I feel lucky to have worked with Bob Lockhart on my first book. His editorial skill is flawlessly paired with speed, efficiency, transparency, and a complete mastery of the publication process, as if tailored specifically to dispel all first book jitters, confusion, or stumbles. He has calmly illuminated and served as guide in the (previously to me) mystical world of book publishing. He magically provided line by line edits in just two weeks as we rushed to copyediting to make sure that my book reached its fullest audience and potential. Working with him and the University of Pennsylvania Press has been a true pleasure from the moment of our first preconference e-mail to the arrival of my completed book in the mailbox.

Of course, any book of history is indebted to the historical actors it traces. However, this book relied on not only their historical actions, but also their present willingness and abilities to help me piece together the history of gay and lesbian health activism in the 1970s. Many provided important pieces of the story simply by sharing their oral histories, or letting a stranger sift through their attics, basements, garages, or backrooms. Without the generosity of Lenny Alberts, Gary Chichester, Sally Deane, Suzanne Gage, Vernita Gray, Donald Kilhefner, Ken Meyer, Mina Meyer, David Ostrow, Sharon Raphael, Karla Rideout, Chuck Renslow, Susan Robinson, David Scondras, Benjamin Teller, Theresa Tobin, Stephen Brophy, Michael Vance, Jane Schwartz, Jerry Feuer, and Francie Hornstein with their time, memories, and papers, as well as the many more who spoke with me off the record, this book truly would never have gotten beyond the brainstorming phase. Walter Lear provided the most inspiring research space I have yet to encounter at the United States Health Left Archive, which at the time was located in his living room. There, I got the unique opportunity to interview a pivotal historical actor and look through all his meticulously kept records (which often were about meetings held in that very room, just forty years earlier) while listening to his longtime partner and former concert pianist, James Payne, play the most beautiful classical piano. Walter passed away in 2010, but his archive lives on at the University of Pennsylvania. Archivists and librarians at the Harvard Libraries, the Northeastern University Snell Library, the Mazer Archives, the Golda Meir Library of the University of Wisconsin–Milwaukee, the ONE Archives, Northwestern University Library, Lambda Archive of San Diego, Schlesinger Library, the Gerber/Hart Library and Archives, the GLAMA Archives in the University of Missouri, Kansas City, the New York Public Library, the Boston Public Library, the History Project Archives in Boston, the Spencer Library at the University of Kansas, and the Young Research Library at the University of California, Los Angeles were incredibly helpful and often pointed my research in new and useful directions as I sought to fill in the gaps and make sense of all the privately held papers and histories.

Over the course of this project, I have been affiliated with four different academic institutions: the University of Illinois at Chicago, Macalester College, Gettysburg College, and the University of Kansas. Each of these contributed meaningfully to this book in financial and personal ways. The History Award, the Provost's Award, the Robert Remini Prize, and the Dean's Scholar Award through the University of Illinois at Chicago paid for many of my early research-related expenses. A four-year scholarship from Point Foundation also allowed me to conduct additional research and draft initial writing. Point Foundation also introduced me to a number of wonderful people who have become mentors and friends. Ken Peoples, Ann Adams, Vince Garcia, Julie Schell, LeLaina Romero, Michelle Marzullo, Ellen Adams, Aaron Ruby, and Carl Streed Jr. have cheered and inspired me throughout the research and writing phases. Macalester College supported my work by allowing me to present ideas in numerous venues, think creatively about how teaching and research fuel one another, and gifting me the friendship of many amazing scholars in the Twin Cities who have played an important role in the shaping of this work. Adrienne Christiansen, Kevin Murphy, Regina Kunzel, Peter Rachleff, Jamie Monson, Herta Wolf Pitman, and Lesley Lavery made my brief time in St. Paul disproportionately meaningful and valuable. Gettysburg College provided me with funding as well as wonderful colleagues in Natalie Cisneros, Cassie Hayes, Nathalie Lebon, Lidia Anchisi, and Kerry Wallach.

My colleagues at the University of Kansas have been invaluable in bringing this project to its full potential. Their feedback in faculty seminars, the Hall Center Gender Seminar, countless conversations, and draft readings has added to the quality and content of my research in ways that I couldn't have expected, but appreciate immeasurably. My colleagues in the Women, Gender, and Sexuality Studies Department have been like a family with many in the American Studies, History, African and African American Studies, and Sociology Departments serving as close cousins as they offered their time, expertise, support, and friendship time and again. The research librarians at Watson Library, particularly Tami Albin, bring a level of expertise I am thankful for every day. Funding through the New Faculty General Research Fund and Friends of the Hall Center Book Publication Award allowed for both the significant restructuring of this book as well as the inclusion of the photographs and a professionally done index. The friendship and gentle mentorship of Alesha Doan, Ann Schofield, Ayesha Hardison, Hannah Britton, Akiko

Takeyama, Charlene Muelenhard, Marta Vicente, Kim Warren, Stacey Vanderhurst, Sarah Deer, Nick Syrett, Shannon Portillo, Erik Scott, Beth Bailey, Sheyda Jahanbani, Andy Denning, Jessica Gerschultz, Sherri Tucker, Clarence Lang, Betsy Esche, Sarah Deer, Jonathan Hagel, David Roediger, Darren Canady, Sally Utech, Juliana Carlson, Giselle Anatol, Katie Rhine, Heba Mostafa, Brian Donovan, Nicole Hodges Persley, and Pam Gordon have kept me focused, supported, and inspired throughout the final drafting and revision of this book. The love of the Hall Center for the Humanities at the University of Kansas is ubiquitous among all humanities faculty here, and I have no doubt that the various forms of support offered to me through its programming, seminars, and funding have made this a better book.

Beyond the institutions that have welcomed me, this work has been shaped in ways both minor and significant by a wonderful network of academics who have been generous with their time and expertise, encouraging of my work, and who have provided additional insight, critique, and scholarship at crucial moments in the development of this work. I would like to thank Claire Potter, Julio Capó Jr., Tim Stewart-Winter, Tamar Carroll, Joanne Meyerowitz, Jonathan Bell, Megan Springate, Nan Boyd, Amber Hollibaugh, Ron Walters, Felicity Northcott, François Furstenberg, Gill Frank, Kevin Mumford, Christina Hanhardt, Cookie Wolner, Don Romesburg, Amanda Littauer, Emily Hobson, Laurel Clark, Alix Genter, Stephen Vider, Marc Stein, LaShonda Mims, Marcia Gallo, Pippa Holloway, Phil Tiemeyer, Tom Foster, Ian Lekus, Estelle Freedman, Milton Wendland, Jen Jack Gieseking, Gayatri Reddy, Lynette Jackson, Cathy Cohen, Sarah Schulman, Dan Royles, Felicity Northcott, Katrin Schultheiss, Eric Arnesen, Leon Fink, Sue Levine, Kevin Schultz, Annelise Orleck, Ian Darnell, Tom Sugrue, Elena Gutiérrez, Barbara Ransby, Leisa Meyer, Corey Capers, AJ Lewis, Monica Mercado, Gabe Rosenberg, Julie Enszer, Cat Jacquet, Stephanie Gilmore, Beth Ritchie, Jonathan Ned Katz, Cynthia Blair, Beth Collins, and Tim Retzloff. Writing groups with Anne Parsons, Lara Kelland, Jessica Gerschultz, and Emily LaBabera-Twarog kept me from getting stuck or feeling lost. It is an honor to be in conversation with each of them. The hospitality of Becci Torrey, Barbara Boros, Aaron Glazer, Zoe Fraade-Blanar, and Rebecca Kaiser also made long research trips to New York, Boston, and Los Angeles much more enjoyable.

Intellectual curiosity and debate only take a project of this length and duration so far; friends and family push, pull, yank, lovingly guide, and provide the sustenance required to bring it across the finish line. Myrl Beam and Emily LaBarbera-Twarog, both exciting scholars themselves, have kept me engaged and fueled my heart and mind since the early days of graduate school. Our almost daily phone conversations are among the most valued moments of my days. I thank them for their love, support, and friendship. Kate Eubank, Keeli Nelson, Erik Scott, Peter Karmen, Juliana Carlson, Cody Case, Jessica Gerschultz, Sheyda Jahanbani, Jonathan Hagel, Whitney Denning, Andy Denning, Saida Bonifield, and Stacey Vanderhurst have all been emotional mainstays without which this book would have been far harder to complete. I am deeply thankful for their friendship and their enjoyment of good food and laughter. Kate Madl, Lori Coomes, Molly Costanzo, Amanda Parrish, Joan Axthelm, Meg Lawley, Chrissy Torrey, Aaron Glazer, and Zoe Fraade-Blanar sent well-timed encouragement from afar. Alex Pastern and her mother, Karen, nurtured my love of history at its earliest stages and helped light my path to graduate school and academia. Alex passed away in 2006 and Karen in 2015, though I still think of them often and the elaborate ice cream sundaes we made when taking breaks from studying AP history. Stephanie Swann remains a source of immeasurable strength and a North Star in my life, as she has been since I first came out when I was thirteen. My gratitude for her and Nancy Kropf knows no bounds.

My parents have been the bedrock of support for me. My mother has shown me the true meaning of perseverance and resilience. My father has taught me to critically engage with the world around me and instilled in me a work ethic that has served me well. My mother, father, and stepmom joined in a chorus of encouragement and love that never wavered. They have always believed in me and pushed me to follow my heart in my life and work. My sister Jen continues to be a great source of inspiration and support for me, as she has been for all of my life. She has taught me the importance of meaningful work and the difference one person can make in the lives of others. My grandfather, Dan Moore Sr., bestowed on me his passion for lifelong learning, which sustained him until his passing in 2010, at the age of ninety-three. My aunt Pattie and uncle Mike have been steady supports in ways both big and small throughout my life, but particularly as I set out on my scholarly journey. In the Magnuson family I have been blessed with another set of parents and siblings who have cheered, loved, and inspired me. I aspire to one day possess the transcendent grace and kindness, even in the midst of the most challenging situations, that Bobbie Magnuson embodies every day. Rod Magnuson passed away as this book was in press. He loved his family with an intensity and completeness that was absolute; I hope my loved ones know that same feeling of unequivocal and fierce devotion. Jen, Jeff, Kim and Bob, Ricci and Mark, Rod and Sue, Jamie and Lindsay, Kylie and Nick, and all their kids make me rich in love and laughter.

Though I did my best to relegate my work and writing to the weekdays and regular business hours, inevitably the book occasionally spilled over into my home life, only to be met by patience, understanding, and love from those closest to me. Maya the Moose, my big-eared bed-hog of a dog, has been a constant companion throughout the entire writing process. I appreciate her willingness to go on walks at a moment's notice so that I could mull over an idea or break through a writing block. I had my son, Elliot, in the midst of the research and drafting of this book. Watching him grow, learn, and navigate the world in his own way for the last seven years reminds me daily to be thankful for the time I have with him and to seize every opportunity to shape a better and more just future for him and his generation. He provides a healthy and important perspective that inspires me both to be the best person I can be and to laugh at myself in the process—a mind-set that I think translates well to the act of writing. My partner, Kellie, fell in love with me despite my many flaws and shortcomings, and then stuck by my side as we moved with a small child from Chicago to St. Paul, rural Pennsylvania, and now, Kansas. Her love and companionship bring balance to my life, challenge my thinking, and push me constantly to grow and learn. She nourishes my soul and makes me a better person. Her passion for social justice helps fuel my own whether on the picket lines of Chicago, at rallies in Topeka, or at the dining room table, where we work across from one another. She enjoys my cooking, makes a mean cocktail, dances with me in the kitchen, and learned to hike in large part because it feeds my soul. I am honored and humbled she chooses to share her life with me and supports me so completely.